NEVERTHELESS

Carolyn E. Kendall

PublishAmerica
Baltimore

First printing

ISBN: 1-4241-6686-1
PUBLISHED BY PUBLISHAMERICA, LLLP
www.publishamerica.com
Baltimore

Printed in the United States of America

Bobbie,

God bless ~~from~~ You!

A Loving Tribute
To
Our Exceptional Son, David

CE Kendall
Luke 22:42

"Father, if Thou art willing, remove
this cup from me. NEVERTHELESS,
not my will, but Thine, be done."
Luke 22:42 RSV

For years, I nurtured in my mind the idea of a book about our exceptional son, David.

David: Strong, enduring the often unendurable.
Inside, a peaceful child.
Outside, no peace at all.
His exterior unpredictably, successfully masking
the gentleness that wanted to surface.
David: Sweet, loving, forgiving.
Sweet, even when other people were unaccountably abusive to him.
Loving, even when others frequently exhibited only hatefulness
toward him.
Forgiving of the failure of us all, to go an extra mile, or to attempt to
walk in his difficult footsteps.
David: A sturdy bough on God's tree, bending in the
continual storms of life, but never breaking!

The Winter of Spring

In the spring of 1982, this book had its beginning as a literary project. My husband and I had returned from a Wednesday night church service, and the evening's topic kept flitting through my thoughts. The minister had briefly spoken about the word, "Nevertheless." I could not stop thinking about it. Somehow, both the Biblical and Webster's definitions seemed to describe our younger son, David.

Dave was thirteen years old that spring, facing not only the "terrible teens," which could be overwhelming to "normal" people, but battling more serious threats to his future. He carried physical, mental and emotional scars of having been born brain-damaged. Not just in a single area, but injured in several, any one of which by itself was serious, and which, combined, made his life—and ours—a nightmare.

Totally speech deficient by the age of two, he had begun daily therapy when he was only twenty-seven months old, gradually progressing from weekly to three-times-a-week with the speech therapist.

Unable to understand abstract concepts, to have a "mind picture" of a situation and then translate it into a "concrete" situation which could be dealt with, he appeared much of the time to be in a daze.

Hyperactive to an almost unbelievable degree, he had been placed at seventeen months of age on increasingly stronger dosages of supposedly therapeutic drugs. Four were tried and three were unsuccessful in helping him stay in one place for more than a few fleeting seconds. As each month passed, his body built a tolerance to the single drug that offered a little help. The more he grew physically, the more massive became the doses of Mellaril.

His inability to grasp mathematics in the simplest forms followed him like a bleak cloud into adulthood, making him an easy target for dishonest store clerks…and others. It also, for many years, put me in charge of paying his adult living expenses out of his own account after a three-year experiment with him in charge of his checking account failed miserably during his teens. Eventually, technology gave him more independence when utility companies became able to make automatic withdrawals from his account…and he gradually realized that a supply of blank checks did not mean that he still had money in the bank!

The extremely slow development of David's gross and fine motor skills frequently made him the laughing stock of peers. Trying as hard possible, he could not catch a ball, hold a pencil, ride a tricycle, walk a balance beam, even draw a circle or hold normal-size toys until long after "normal" children accomplished the activities.

In the late 1960s and early '70s, there were very few places to turn for help with a child such as David. It sounds archaic now, but children with deficiencies such as David's were most often dealt with by "putting them away." There were so pitifully few competent diagnostic tools and trained personnel available, let alone words of comfort and encouragement for the innocent victims and their families.

Friends and family offered only half-hearted, if any, pledges of help. It appeared that they hoped any offers would not be accepted. Mostly, there was a litany of predictions of doom, followed by "I told you so" when those predictions too often became harsh reality.

I wondered then, as now, if it would have been easier for our small family to face the daily challenges with David, if someone had come to us and said, "I've been there too. I believe I understand what you are seeing in your lives. Yes, I do know the pain which there can be, for the child and family, alike. Don't give up! Have courage enough to face not only today, but also those entirely unknown tomorrows that may be even worse. And, face them, no matter what they bring."

After years of facing them, in that spring of 1982, I began chronicling David's uphill struggle for survival. Perhaps his story of overcoming the unwelcome challenges might provide some hope for other people in similar circumstances.

That single word, "NEVERTHELESS," provided the impetus for me to begin…to face my word processor, to face our experiences and, however difficult, to face my own feelings.

From birth, David exhibited a "nevertheless" type of behavior. He seemed to wish with all of his being to be able to change the challenges, to do away with the brain damage and all that stood between him and every goal he set. Assuredly, he longed that dealing with the brain damage had never been a reality for him, and us.

All of his wishful thinking changed nothing. Reality had to be faced. Most of the challenges, at least at first glance, appeared to be insurmountable.

NEVERTHELESS, David did his best, not only to face them, but even more, to overcome them!

He set his MIND on a far-off finish line…which goal was, and is, to become a useful adult, a person with marketable skills and a well-earned sense of self-worth. He wanted to prove that he not only had a REASON, but a RIGHT TO EXIST!

He set his HEART on victory:

"…and the
third day I reach my GOAL,
NEVERTHELESS, I must journey on today
and tomorrow and the next day…"
Luke 13:33 New ASB

Jesus, in the Garden of Gethsemane, in the agony and the entirely human dread of what lay ahead in the next few hours, pleaded with the Father, "If it be possible, let this cup pass…**NEVERTHELESS,**" He obediently ended His prayer, "not my will, but Thine be done."

This, too, has been David's prayer, "If it be possible, let this cup pass…**NEVERTHELESS**…"

This is his life, his story. David's road has, most often, been one of terrified travel into unknown circumstances which even the best-trained professionals could neither understand nor predict an outcome.

His story is one of coping with the indecision of medical and educational professionals, while deciding for himself to become more than anyone dared dream. David's journey begins.

PROLOGUE

"I'm sorry, Mrs. Kendall," the doctor began, "but I really believe that you and your husband should consider placing David in an institution. He will probably never be able to go to school. I don't believe that I can be of any help!"

The half-size exam room began to close in on me.

Brusque. Determined. Self-assured.

How very POSITIVE that doctor appeared.

He was so secure—so sure of himself and his own competency to diagnose WITHOUT the benefit of a medical examination...after all, he had been in this room less than five minutes and already had rendered his medical decision about our four-year-old son.

The irony of that scene would replay thousands of times in my mind during the next few years: The doctor, impressively trailed by professional credentials and adoring fourth-year medical students, closed the door on David's future as quickly as he shut that paint-peeling wooden door.

On the far side of the suffocating, tiny room, there I was: stunned, heartbroken, a mother clutching her young son...unable to acknowledge what I had just been told. The pain of hearing it was deafening to my ears. Briefly, my mind closed, and then my defense mechanism sprang into action!

This was UNACCEPTABLE!

I had an uneasy feeling that I was expected to not question this doctor's decision. I was expected to merely stand quietly in awe of this experienced medical person and his pronouncement!

Years older, and medical volumes wiser than I, with his assessment and benediction rolled into those three sentences of doom for David, the doctor turned on his heel and exited.

Six paces behind was his white-coated entourage. For their part, the students-soon-to-be-real-doctors cast sympathetic glances in the direction of David before scurrying away to some other, perhaps more hopeful, pediatric situation.

Wanting to scream, cry, or just jump out of the window as the finality of his decision jolted me, I wondered what could I do to get his attention? Why couldn't he, or the students, or SOMEONE, ANYONE, UNDERSTAND?

How could that doctor be so cruel?

Lord, how could he be so unfeeling?

Briefly rooted in place by this latest, most unexpected insult, I paused. A few seconds seemed to pass as an hundred years.

Suddenly, harder than I intended, I grabbed David by the hand and started running down the corridor of the dilapidated teaching hospital.

We were chasing the doctor! Maybe, if we could get his attention again, he'd change his answer. Maybe, he'd actually do an examination, ask some questions, read some of our child's extensive medical history, find out about David.

Fleetingly hopeful, I mistakenly thought he might even give me some encouragement.

He has to give us some hope. We can't let David's life end before it begins. We came here only for an exam, not a death sentence! How can this be happening?

Thoughts tumbled over each other, as I half-carried, half-dragged our stumbling child toward an evasive exit.

Confused, I had turned down the wrong hall and we were lost in a maze of identical exam rooms and official-looking medical personnel. Rational for a few seconds, I decided to ask for advice before spending the rest of the day just trying to get to the parking lot. The doctor and his group had become history, vanishing into unknown rooms and hallways.

The young male intern who pointed us in the proper direction for the parking lot appeared familiar, as did his name tag. In a strange coincidence, he had been working in the infirmary at Oklahoma State University recently, and had examined my husband, George, a fourth-year veterinary medical student.

Amazingly, the intern recalled our last name. He asked about my husband's recovery, and his class work. Relieved, I felt that I had found a friendly person in a decidedly hostile territory. He accompanied me to the correct door and I asked about the doctor who had just attempted to destroy not only my day, but also David's future.

"Sorry, there is nothing I can suggest. Once a person has had an appointment with HIM, that's just about as far as you can go. He's the top of the ladder around here."

Big help! Thanks, anyway. What a way to conclude four hours of waiting.

David and I had been cooped up in the abbreviated room at Children's Hospital, Oklahoma City, for what seemed an endless time that morning. And, this was not the first time that we'd been waiting for this doctor's expert appraisal. This day, as twice previously, we had been ushered into the small space that was used as an exam room…and left alone.

No one even opened the door to see if we were still there. Hours passed. Hope alternated with foreboding, as footsteps made their way past the door and then became silent.

This was the very same room where we had waited on two other occasions. Each wait had ended in vain, even though we had appointments.

Considering the history, this particular room didn't seem to be a good omen.

On an earlier visit, we were informed that the staff "just forgot" about us. That may be a feat easy to accomplish in a training hospital where thousands of patients are briefly seen, mostly for the benefit of doctors-in-training.

Of course, the lower fees were the biggest reason people used this service. That was certainly our main reason, as we had no money for consultation with a private practitioner.

March 1973 meant graduation was approaching for my husband, a senior student at Oklahoma State University's College of Veterinary Medicine. We lived in Stillwater, a 140-mile round-trip from Children's Hospital in Oklahoma City. Even at pre-embargo gasoline prices, it was difficult for our meager budget to afford one trip, much less the three that had been made.

However, financial fees were not the only costs extracted. We felt that we paid emotionally far more than we paid in dollars for the two hospital trips that ended with no exam being done.

As if that were not bad enough, George had taken a day off from classes when we made our first futile trip. That was a luxury he could ill afford, with national and state board exams only six weeks away.

The second and third trips, David and I went alone. However, without George's moral support, those hospital vigils, waiting on non-existent exams and diagnoses, were even more upsetting.

We suspected, at the very least, there was a serious time management problem for the hospital when the second exam failed to materialize and a medical student announced that the doctor was too busy to see David. After all, we had only been waiting for three hours, and it must have taken a while to track us down in our increasingly familiar exam room. Didn't they know sooner that he "was busy" so that we could not have been delayed?

Now, during the latest four-hour wait, I began to wonder if the ravenous old building were simply devouring patients and doctors alike, and somehow the outside world was failing to notice?

George and I had hoped that this third trip would be charmed and at the very least the specialist would perform an exam on David. Surely, we would be granted some sort of "audience" with The Doctor.

In spite of being ignored the previous two times, hope did not die easily for us.

At least, not until The Doctor made his appearance.

Our family, including even our six-year-old, John, felt in varying degrees that during this final time we would be given some answers. If no answers were given, we could not afford a fourth trip.

Outside the hospital, here and there small clumps of the dying winter of 1973 remained, with melting snow tracing unsure sketches across the landscape. The scene briefly darkened as a cloud found its way in front of the brave sun. The gloomy emptiness in my heart swelled, then disappeared.

"Well, David, we can't stand here with me crying and you looking so sad. We've got to find the car, drive that seventy miles home…and start all over! There's nothing here for us but, maybe, somewhere else, another time…another doctor…"

Saying that out loud was one thing. Believing it was something altogether different.

Even as I fought against their appearance, bitter, angry thoughts re-surfaced.

Look, Carolyn, I was thinking, you've had hope. Forget it. It doesn't really exist, certainly not for David. You've been crazy these past four years, to even think of having hope!

I tried to bury the negative thoughts. Instead, they drummed insistently between my ears. *What a cruel joke has been played on David! He's the victim of a misfortune that was not his fault… There's not even a person or thing that can be blamed! No satisfaction in that! We just have to accept the awful truth…and, maybe, I never have accepted the whole truth!* Rapid-fire thoughts tumbled through my mind.

Maybe all those other doctors who've seen and examined him were right. Maybe, too, the friends and relatives who've said, "Give him back to the adoption agency where you got him" were just trying to save us some grief!

"But, what about David? He's the one with the problems and we MUST help him!"

How often I'd repeated that statement!

It seemed to be a frequent exercise—trying to convince myself that we were actually doing the right thing.

The light of the slowly warming, near-spring day shed a few beams on my thinking, clearing out one or two darkened corners. I forced myself to admit that, perhaps, I had been so blinded by my mother role and mother-love that I had refused to see reality.

"Lord, what if I have been wrong all along?"

Even worse: "Four years of working with him, sacrificing and trying to help him…often ignoring George and little John, in order to 'make things better' for David. Hoping, praying…now it may all be going down the drain."

Self-admonishment consumed my attention as we walked across the full parking lot.

"Surely, some of the other doctors, who saw him in the last four years, knew SOMETHING!"

THAT thought was certainly no comfort. It merely reinforced my own stubbornness.

This day had started so hopefully. We awakened very early, placing all thoughts on what the outcome of the exam might be. Full of anticipation, we believed that "Today we'll finally know what the next steps are, to help David."

Valiant flowers were trying to bloom in our yard. George had the prospect of a job following graduation and hope was literally springing up around us.

My thoughts began to react positively as I remembered how the day had begun.

"Surely, it will be worth these three trips…and all the waiting," I had mused.

At the hospital, David had occupied himself by scrawling pictures on the dusty floor of the exam room.

"This time we're gonna see The Doctor. He will examine David and give us a diagnosis…maybe tentative, but a diagnosis."

I mentally applauded our endurance in having made this third appointment.

Yessir…Now we were going to Find Out Something!

Wrong!

Waiting…as seconds crept into eons…and David became more hyperactive. In itself, his activity wasn't so bad, as it distracted my less pleasant thoughts: *What IF we don't see the doctor, again, this time? What IF?…what if…*

The exam room may have been in the pediatric section of the hospital, but there were no child-friendly playthings in sight. The only objects in this now familiar room were dusty remnants of dog-eared books for children, plus a few scraps of paper and broken bits of crayon…all forlorn and long since forgotten in a cigar box, of all things, bleakly occupying a small space on the top shelf of the lonely bookcase.

Knowing about these items, and lack of "kid stuff," I had put a few creative items in my purse as we were leaving home. I tried to interest my son in pencil, paper, his favorite books and some storytelling.

It didn't work.

Bored and tired, we amused ourselves with the one "redeeming" feature of our entrapment: a greasy window, through which we could see the foggy outlines of hospital traffic. Four-wheeled and two-footed, it passed in review.

Observing that vague parade was not an easy accomplishment. Windowpanes, testifying to years of inattention by what must have been an almost nonexistent janitorial staff, tempted me to print messages across them: "Help! I'm a prisoner in here" or "I last saw your world in 1900!"

Briefly amused, I tried diverting David's attention, and that developed into a battle of wits.

Energetic to a nearly unbelievable extent, David exhausted me even when he was sitting still because something was always in motion: head, hands, arms, legs, feet, fingers. Trying to keep up with his busy little body in our cubicle, while the hours slowly passed wore on my ingenuity and nervous system in equal parts. Physical and emotional tiredness embraced me.

We had settled in for The Wait.

Now, suddenly, The Wait had ended!

Like this?

This disappointment?

This FINAL BLOW?

THIS DOCTOR?

Hope drained from me. Why even bother now? After all, The Doctor was NUMBER ONE in his field of pediatric neuropsychiatry in a large geographic area, highly recommended and The Answer to the prayers of many parents.

No exam?

No testing? What kind of "number one doctor" was he, anyway?

Nothing that he did that afternoon appeared to me to give him a basis for his hasty "diagnosis."

The tone of finality in his voice effectively, though thankfully only temporarily, wiped out hope for David, for our family.

Watching as The Doctor and his troupe left, I was suddenly suffocated with anxiety and fear. Chasing after him, becoming lost, hearing the opinion of the intern...it was too much!

I made another grab for David's hand and lunged out the door.

Having had the proper exit pointed out, David and I raced past more medical students, whose faces registered curiosity and surprise...then we passed less-curious nurses and patients.

Tears started.

We dashed past the glass and brass doors, and, finally we were FREE of that place!

Tears were now stinging my eyes. Droplets slithered down the only decent jacket I owned...onto the top of David's soft, dark-blond hair. Our child and I clung to each other. We embraced the beckoning spring day, the unsure weeks, months and lifetime ahead.

Passersby stared.

Who cared?

We didn't!

What could those other people know of our feelings?

As my hysteria subsided, my bewildered and frightened child murmured, "Momma, what's wrong? Momma, are you sick?" And, most damning, "Momma, are you crying because of ME?"

Still crying on the outside and screaming on the inside, I eventually located our six-year-old car. As I fumbled for the keys, I felt a gentle tug on my skirt.

David's small, scared voice called softly, again and again, "Momma, what's wrong? Is it ME?"

I opened the door, helped Dave scoot in and fasten his seat belt. Then, exhausted, I dropped into the driver's seat.

Too mentally wrung out to drive or think, I simply sat…and sat. I reached for David, unfastened his seat belt and held him again.

I wanted to be able to confront the anxieties and make sense of a seemingly senseless situation. How could I face anything when I felt so helpless?

So, we sat. And waited. Time was passing. So?

So was David's life…passing seemingly into nothingness.

Finally, I attempted to answer David's question.

While I had been wrestling for answers for him, our sweet son had remained quietly seated. Even in the confusion of the past few hours and the upheaval of the last few minutes, he had managed to remain unusually quiet. A miracle!

Perhaps he could feel some of the burden of the moment and could sense that I was unable to face him. He blessedly seemed to sense that he should now stay silent.

My answer, when it was ready for him at last, probably made as little sense to our four-year-old as anything possibly could: "No, Son, it's NOT you! It's the PEOPLE who don't understand you and your problems. Those people don't really seem to care, either, honey. Right now, our problem, yours and mine, is to not pay attention to them. We just have to find our own answers and we will have to work things out by ourselves. David, it's going to take you, me, Daddy and John. Most of all, it's gonna take God, to handle our problems. It's up to Him and to us, the way it REALLY ALWAYS HAS BEEN since the first time we held you in our arms."

I felt overwhelming anger, frustration and sadness, for David, for our family and for myself.

Strange as it may seem, I carried a guilty feeling about David and his problems…unreasonable guilt, laid on me by usually well-meaning medical professionals and reinforced by close relatives and friends.

It was unreasonable, inasmuch as I knew that I had no part in David's yet-to-be-defined problems. Still, I kept getting blamed for them!

Self-control swept away in a flood of emotions and tears. Again.

The dam had burst! Tears started. Refused to stop.

How many times would this keep happening, the pumped-up false hope concluding in turmoil?

Out of who-knows-what-reasoning, fear or empathy, David's tears joined mine. It had been a difficult day for him, too.

For long moments we sat…I, with shattered hope and desolation covering me; David, with no way to understand the enormous problems facing him and us…a child staring through his tear-filled eyes, mystified by a world that might never be his. Even now, years later, as I recall that day and our feelings, and as I type neat letters across the blank screen, that wrenching pain returns:

I cannot keep back the tears.

It hurt then.

It hurts now.

CHAPTER ONE
The Puzzle Begins

"Time flies when you're having fun." What a crazy thought, I mused, stepping over and around boxes.

"Boy, this is NOT going to be easy—or fast—getting settled, again," I reminded myself for the hundredth time.

"Five years of packing and undoing SHOULD have given me enough experience...somehow...to do a great deal better than THIS," I scolded myself as I surveyed the moving-day mess.

Daydreaming was partly to blame for my lethargy.

"How can so much time have passed, without it SEEMING to be that long," randomly occurred to me, as I dug into another box.

My hand had touched the corner of a picture frame. As I pulled away the carefully wrapped newspaper protecting it, I saw, once more, the beaming bridal couple that we had been, just ending our walk up the aisle into a new life. Encouraged by the photographer, we had continued past the last pews and out the front door of the church. We paused as I answered the photographer's question to me, "What's your name?"...WRONG ANSWER! After all, I'd only had my new name a very few minutes!

Laughing, George and I turned toward each other, and the film captured forever the happiness and amusement of the moment.

Starry-eyed, and full of plans, we were, on that December 1962 evening. Mutual friends had introduced us only four brief months earlier. Although marriage was not high on our list of priorities when we met, George had launched a whirlwind (and frequently erratic) courtship.

Tall, dark haired, good-looking, energetic and interesting, he had captured my attention. We soon discovered that we shared many goals and ideals. It wasn't long before we realized that our lives were going to be spent together.

"For better or for worse..." Well, certainly we agreed that it had been "for better" at least up to this point, September 1968.

Shortly before we married, George had received his degree in business administration from Oklahoma State University, and within a couple of months after our wedding he started to work for Ralston Purina Company. We quickly moved from our garage apartment in Oklahoma City to Garden City in southwestern Kansas.

His position was as a district sales manager in animal nutrition. Often away from home and busy until long after regular hours, George encouraged me to travel with him.

Finding my housework in the small four-plex apartment completed in a minimal amount of time and wanting to feel that I was a part of his work, I did travel with him much of the time. I found myself doing record-keeping as well as lettering the large posters he used in his monthly sales meetings for dealers and their employees.

We became friends with his associates, integrating our lives with theirs, settling into somewhat of a routine for a couple of years, assuming that we'd have a family someday.

Soon, however, medical testing showed that pregnancy might be impossible and could even present serious problems both for me and for any child I might conceive. The alternative of adoption was considered and accepted. We made application with Lutheran Social Service in Wichita, Kansas.

On June 1, 1966, at the conclusion of nine months of interviews and tests that dredged into our lives and finances, we welcomed our first adopted son, William John, six days after his May 26th birth.

Now that we were parents, we naively anticipated years of a peaceful family life...working together and rearing our child.

Early 1967 found George being transferred to northeastern Oklahoma. He had done so well in his Kansas assignment, building up an area which had previously not prospered, that he was given another lackluster district. He could, once again, prove his ability to train, promote, motivate and challenge dealers to do more than they thought they could!

The built-in "thorn" in this rose, however, was a decrease in salary until the sales increased. When sales did increase, he would have a renewal of his commission. All told, in spite of the thorns, we agreed to give it a try. In a few months, profitability was growing for the company as well as for us.

In the spring of 1968, we felt that things were doing amazingly and we could apply for adoption of another infant. Girl or boy, it did not matter. We just hoped that this latest addition would be as healthy and outgoing as our first child.

Just sit back, relax, be comfortable, and let life roll along.

That *sounded* idyllic, but it wasn't about to happen!

In June, his boss presented my husband with the prospect of yet another "promotion." This time, the wisdom of five years' experience gave us several second thoughts: How long would THIS move take, to build up another district to profitability; what about the next move...and the next?

We seriously wondered why it seemed that every time George's income reached a livable level, the company almost immediately pared it down. Was this going to continue to be the trend, in spite of promises to the contrary by George's superiors?

We had enjoyed the challenges of his sales/ nutritional consulting career. However, the questions about continually uprooting, rebuilding someone else's failing district and George's ongoing contact with the animal industry, began to turn our thoughts in another direction...toward veterinary medicine.

He had been interested in that field for years and we now faced a decision of major proportions: Should he continue with Purina with the uncertainty we felt it would bring, or should he quit everything and return to OSU to become a veterinarian...with the equal uncertainty of that situation?

We doggedly assembled all of the practical excuses we could muster to NOT return to college. The biggest reason was our twenty-five-month-old son, John, who needed the security that the adoption agency rightly assumed we would provide.

The dream of becoming a veterinarian soon overrode all of the negatives we could find. We meshed our desires and dreams into The Plan: George would return to school. And, somehow, we would survive.

Not live, mind you. Just survive.

And, that's just about what it eventually came down to.

Many prayers, and much soul-searching, brought us into family unity in our determination that he should reach his goal. We sold our lovely new home and had a three-bedroom, twelve-foot-wide, sixty-four-foot long mobile home custom-built. Thus, a very different life began in approximately 720 square feet, at George's alma mater at Stillwater, Oklahoma.

All-too-painfully aware that our savings and funds from the sale of our home would not last as long as school, we tried to prepare ourselves for the sub-poverty existence awaiting us.

As importantly, medical students had such academic demands on their time that we knew there would be very few moments for family life. In addition, there would be no time for him to have a job, other than his monthly Army Reserve duty as a captain and commander of Company B, Stillwater. He would go on active duty in the summers for whatever time the military would allow, but always thirty days or less. Anything more would change his status and amount of pay.

As an educated, trained and experienced journalist, I might have gone to work, except that we agreed that I would not work away from home. More important than anything was our young John, who needed me with him more than we thought that we needed grocery money.

We would manage.

And our child: toddling, learning, with his bright blue eyes aglow at each new accomplishment, was the light of each of our days. He brought joy and happiness into our lives. In fact, he had been such a delight, that the decision to adopt a second child was very easily made. In March we had started the adoption process again...and August 31st was the last day that George worked for Purina.

Adoptions are not inexpensive now, nor were they in 1968. When my husband's employment plans changed and George headed back to OSU, we told the agency. We had thought that we might no longer be considered very good prospects as adoptive parents, as our finances would be severely limited. However, the agency took a generous point of view: They reduced our fees to a minimum and our social worker continued his pre-placement interviews with us during the summer.

...RING!

I was jarred from my reverie. Time to answer the phone, then get back to unpacking

The phone is unpacked, or it couldn't be ringing, I thought as I hunted in vain for it.

Why can't the phone just calm down? I'm doing the best I can, crawling across boxes to answer it. Maybe whoever is calling will just give up. Doggone it, h-a-n-g u-p! Try again when I'm not so BUSY!

RING!

What insanity prompted us to make this blasted decision, anyway? I silently complained as I tripped over yet another box.

I caught myself on my elbows, scraping my arm on a sharp-edged crate. OUCH!

"Not even moved in and already this silly trailer is too small! For THIS we gave up income and some kind of security and a beautiful home…all of those important things? For THIS?"

I surveyed the havoc from my sprawled vantage point.

The phone refused to silence itself.

And, the dumbest thing, I assured myself, *is the absolute uncertainty. Sure, sure, George has all of those credits in science and math. Yes, I KNOW he's already finished nearly all of the classes he needs to apply to vet school.*

Yeah, but he still has to complete this year and finish up a couple of the required courses. He's got to make super grades. Then, he can finally apply for vet school…

The elusive phone continued to sound off from its hiding place.

After application, there're the interviews with the admission committee…Lord, maybe more than one or two interviews…and the weeks or months of waiting to find out if he's even been accepted.

All of that…with no assurance that he WILL be accepted!

RING-G-G-G!

There are only forty-eight places in the first year class…competition is tough…and someone told us that more than 600 people have applied…

RING-G-G-G-G-G-G!

Mr. Bell's invention urgently bleated its reminder…

Who on earth would stay on the phone for such a long time? And, why?

The latest jangling spurred me to make one last desperate jump over the final hurdle.

I lunged at the noisy phone, which was barely exposed under a stack of wadded newspaper packing. Doubting that the caller had the patience to still be on the line, I swept the receiver up, half expecting to hear the dial tone.

Instead, a friendly, familiar voice excitedly announced, "This is Lutheran Social Service. Your new son wants to see you!"

Oh, Lord, I silently prayed, *please tell me that we made the right decision about continuing the adoption application.*

It did occur to me that my prayer might just be a trifle belated! Stammering into the mouthpiece, I tried to match the social worker's enthusiasm, "That's wonderful! When can we come after him?"

"Tomorrow!"

"Tomorrow?"

Galvanized into action, George and I literally tore into the remaining boxes for a few hours, stringing belongings and thoughts throughout our tiny new home.

We often rescued John from the confines of emptied packing crates and tried to get ready for the 900-mile round trip to Rainbow Street, Kansas City, Kansas. (I have always thought it very sweet to find a baby under the rainbow…that beats finding a pot of gold by a long shot!)

Newborn David would be ours. Tomorrow!

He was the same six days of age that John had been when our first child came into our home and hearts. Remembering the beautiful feelings of that first occasion gave us heroic energy. We readied ourselves and left late that afternoon.

As we settled into the car, weighted with paraphernalia for two children, George and I exchanged thoughts. "After all," we wondered, "how much more difficult can TWO sons be, than one?"

Fortunately, for all of us, we had no idea about the answer!

Expecting to see a small newborn, we were shocked the next morning by the sheer volume of David! The baby was the usual pink-tinged, red-faced, lusty-lunged infant. Weighing over nine pounds, he looked weeks, rather than days, old. He had reddish hair, blue eyes…and a strange-looking vertical knot between his eyes.

The knot increased in size and turned an angry reddish-purple when he cried….which he was vigorously doing when we first saw him.

A warning cloud flitted across my mind.

I dismissed the anxious feeling, attributing it to the nervous realization that we were now the parents of two.

Also, our very long trip was only half-completed. And, George had to start classes tomorrow!

Worn out from moving, traveling and lack of sleep, I found lots of logical reasons for feeling apprehensive. We accompanied the social worker, with our two sons, to a nearby Lutheran church, where we formally accepted responsibility for this new member of our family.

With our permission, a large group of parochial school children gave their wide-eyed attention to the "Placement Service" as they sensed that something very special was taking place and they were the fortunate observers.

The impressive ritual, conducted by the minister at the altar of his church, haunts and challenges us still today:

"...Do you desire to take this child, George David Kendall, for your own? Will you be to him a true father and mother, in spirit and in deed? Will you show him love...understanding...Give him companionship and guidance...Treat him with patience and forbearance...Receive this child now, in the Name of Jesus, as a gift, and as a trust from God, who would have you bring him up as your son, in His fear and love..."

Obediently, solemnly, we answered each question affirmatively, "We will."

With faith in God and in each other, we so easily committed ourselves, our sons and our future. Mercifully, there was no inkling that our dreams were already turning into nightmares.

Unknowingly, we committed ourselves to strife, disappointment, discouragement and unbelievable pain.

Praise God, we also, unknowingly committed ourselves to a stronger family bond, to individual spiritual growth, to caring and sharing.

This was a commitment to love. And, not wanting to break the solemnity of the moment, I kept a private thought, smiling as I considered the impact of what they had witnessed on the young children in the chapel. I could visualize the moment when they dashed into their various homes that evening, and quizzed their parents, "Mom! Dad! Do you know how you get babies? They give 'em away at church!"

That thought still makes me smile!

CHAPTER TWO
Our Lives Unravel

"But, I've tried everything and I don't know anything else to do!"

In desperation, with my patience at an end, I shoved sixteen-day-old David into his father's arms. Until today, our new son had been relatively calm. Suddenly, for no apparent reason, he began to scream at the top of his lungs.

And scream.

And scream.

My nervous system dissolved.

Nothing that I could think of soothed him.

Not one of my efforts made the slightest difference.

He didn't seem to be sick. Or hungry. And, he didn't need another diaper.

In spite of his swallowing great gulps of air during his outbursts, no colic seemed to be bothering him.

Even a baby enema didn't help!

Rocking wasn't the answer.

Neither was my singing, which due to lack of talent, probably made things slightly worse.

Walking the floor, talking to the baby, turning the radio on, and off, turning the television on, and off, nothing hushed his agonized cries.

Nothing changed the powerful, wild sounds bellowing forth from his tiny, innocent-appearing mouth. Not even a trip to the pediatrician's office changed the quality or quantity of the ear-splitting volume. Except, naturally, when the doctor entered the room!

Then, for the first time in hours, David became as quiet as he could be. Not a murmur.

The doctor probably thought that I was overreacting to the new baby by simply imagining that David cried continually. He indicated as much while politely patting my arm, suggesting that "the baby's actions really could not have been as dreadful" as I had related to him.

Yeah, right!

However, the instant we left the office building and reached our car, David's squalling began bouncing off the sidewalks, louder than ever.

Thanks a lot, doctor, I thought, as I belted the baby and his carrier into the back seat.

At home, the Sound War continued. Eardrum-piercing-level was knifing through the shreds of my sanity.

Toddler John managed to cover his own ears, first with his small hands, then with his small pillow, trying to muffle the sounds.

Hours passed. John and I tried to ignore David, a move that was doomed from the start. Ignore the sound of a tornado? Probably not!

Finally, we tucked him into his crib, closed the door, and let him rage into sleepiness.

The nap lasted at least five minutes, at which time our exhausted student-father-husband practically crawled in from class. Mentally crawled, that is. Physically, he was bushed. Emotionally, he was beaten. Mentally, he had had it! A very long day at school. An equally long evening was facing him as he tackled the incredible stack of homework.

"We've had quite a day, too, honey. Lots of homework here, you know. Meals, dishes, laundry, children, the pediatrician..."

Ignoring my sarcasm, George moved books and notes onto the dining table, looking for a quiet place to study.

The table certainly was not that place!

It was only the width of one-eighth inch of plywood distance from our screaming infant's room to the kitchen. The walls were not exactly soundproofed. And, the trailer walls didn't touch the floor properly. They just skimmed along with frequent air and sound spaces. Noise flooded through and under the inadequate barrier between David's small room and George's study area in the kitchen.

Fifteen minutes of organizing pens, paper and books, sharpening pencils and listening, had George logically asking, "Can't you do something to make David calm down?"

Illogically, I retorted, "I've run out of ideas! The doctor is no help at all! I've listened to David's crying for six hours while you were gone! Now, you try to do something!"

John watched, with big-eyed interest, as our verbal stew began to boil, accompanied by the wails on the other side of the adjoining wall.

Storming away thirty feet to the far end of the trailer, I hoped to put some sound-absorbing distance between my husband, children and myself.

Too tired and frustrated to care how I sounded, I hollered over the infant's continuing tirades, "You might try putting a pillow over his head!"

No, I didn't mean it, but I felt defeat engulfing me. The noise had been going on for hours. The failure I was feeling suffocated any desire that I might have had to face this latest problem in our already disrupted lives.

Worse, I was starting to feel cut off, not only from my small family, but from God.

The popular quote "If God seems far away, guess who moved?" didn't enter my mind. I simply ached with a premonition of abandonment. In a home occupied by three other people, I felt so ALONE.

A very real fear chilled me.

What was happening to us?

Were we now going to drift aimlessly along, not knowing what to do for a child who would not respond to our best efforts?

What WAS the point of this?

Self-pity moved in. Fast!

One thought led to another: "Lord, how long is this going to last? Why is David crying so much? Lord, what are You doing to us? Do You even hear me?"

To my surprise, I heard my last pitiful plea ALOUD, instead of in my thoughts, as my crying joined David's. Until then, I hadn't realized that I was speaking out loud.

Hearing me and thinking that I was pleading with him, George picked up the phone, dialing the home of our pediatrician. Back in those days, doctors actually had their home phones listed in the directory.

During the brief conversation with David's doctor, who wanted to get back to his dinner table, my husband heard a repetition of the statement made to me earlier that day: "I know of nothing to calm your son. I don't believe the child has a problem, really. If he does, I don't know the cause of it. Thank you. Good night."

"Well...We don't know the cause either, or if there is a problem...doctor," George growled into the phone.

In a swift move, before the pediatrician could hang up, George grabbed David, holding the loudly protesting bundle next to the receiver, giving the M.D. a full blast of the child's efficient lung-power!

THAT got some results!

Especially as it was accompanied by George's promise to drop David off at the *doctor's home* immediately, for overnight observation, and diagnosis!

Amazingly quickly, the doctor suggested that we "bundle" our baby.

"Maybe that will help."

Bundle?

We had no idea what he meant.

We'd never heard of it, but after the doctor's brief explanation, we tried it...and it worked!

In fact, it worked for weeks!

David actually calmed down.

When he would begin screaming, he would pull his little arms and legs into a prenatal position. Clinching his small fists and doubling his little legs up next to his diaper only increased the tension in the rest of his body. Soon, he would not be able to relax. All he could do was bleat out his vocal battle against the world.

"Bundling" was forced relaxation. It consisted of placing the vermilion-faced infant on a receiving blanket, straightening out his folded arms and legs, then rolling him snugly in the blanket. Next, we would secure the blanket edges with large safety pins so that he could not kick free. Our miniature "mummy" looked rather strange, with only his head emerging from the colorful blanket. Strange, and, mercifully, peaceful.

The unexpected sound of silence was wonderful.

Battered by David's unceasing sounds for nearly twenty-four constant hours, we now gratefully savored the pleasant, peaceful, restful silence. In near disbelief, we watched as David slipped into a normal sleep, interrupted only by his feeding demands.

For the next five weeks, we bundled our baby, until he outgrew the receiving blankets...and, perhaps, his need to be so closely secured.

Ten o'clock each evening would find us repeating the odd bedtime procedure. For some reason that we did not understand, late evening was the time when David would begin his worst raging.

Apparently, without some assistance, his body was less able to relax at that time of day. Maybe, there was some routine that his biological mother had followed to which his built-in clock was still responding. We would never know.

What we did observe was that there was an overwhelming need of some sort for his little body to be enveloped in the blanket.

This was all the more puzzling, because after that first terrible twenty-four hours, David usually seemed all right during the daytime.

At least for a while.

Normal routines followed each other throughout our day. We held, loved, fed, entertained and cuddled David. For the most part, David responded the way John had when he was an infant.

However, at 10:00 p.m., Jekyll and Hyde reversed! The rampages would get underway, stopping only when the last safety pin was in place on the blanket.

John lovingly gave all of the two-year-old help that he could devise. He showed concern and love for his little brother. The screaming sibling didn't dampen John's enthusiasm and hopes for a playmate. Our sensitive and gifted toddler, hardly more than a baby himself, tried to rock and calm his brother. He was undaunted, even when his best efforts, and ours, were fruitless.

My husband and I realized that our older son's visions of having a companion, baseball pitcher, pirate hunter and fellow butterfly-chaser were probably fading fast.

Young John wanted David to "hurry up and get big 'nuff to run, play, help me draw and sing, ride uh bike and climb trees, an' go fishin' with Dad."

"Yes, John."

A little boy's dreams.

He sincerely believed that the two of them would be able to tackle life headlong, and cross the goal line, together.

John wanted David to be his "bes' fren' ," one with whom he could challenge the world, while they mutually defended each other from outside peer pressure.

Years have passed since those childhood dreams were expressed. Life became tougher for each of our sons. Those dreams eventually faded and drifted into memories.

CHAPTER THREE
More Complications

It was almost impossible to keep our two active children even moderately calm during the long hours that George needed to spend studying at home. On one hand, we had an exploring, creative, two-and-a-half-year-old who spent every waking minute discovering something new and wonderful in our 720-square-foot-world. The limited interior space was even more cramped than we had anticipated, when we chose mobile life over renting.

On the other hand, there was David. Loud David. Busy David. Crying David. Demanding David. Sparkly-eyed and sweetly smiling David. Chubby-faced and endearing to the fullest, when he wasn't howling about some unknown misdemeanor that had upset him.

Noisy, nonetheless.

Then, there was Carolyn: wife, mother, typist for Daddy's unending papers and projects…mostly tired all of the time.

And, there was George, trying to keep mind and body going in the same direction, exhaustion being the only physical state with which he was to be acquainted for many years.

Now, looking at snapshots made shortly before David's birth, others taken the day we received him from the adoption agency…and, still more, snapped a brief few weeks and months later, a drastic change is obvious. George and Carolyn…especially Carolyn…look like vastly different people.

Somewhere, in those few short months, my smile was replaced by a sad, dreary expression. It stayed there much too long, as succeeding photos testify. There seemed to be little to smile about. Days passed in a blur of diapers, dishes, bottles and books, studying and struggling. We simply tried to survive.

George scurried around during his limited, precious moments away from books, found some used lumber that wasn't too expensive and started construction on a study room.

His "outhouse," although not the traditional kind, was to provide him much-needed space where he could have *quiet* in which to study.

The tiny building had only enough room for a desk, which was actually a wooden table purchased at a saloon auction during his first years in college (and complete with carved initials of long-gone imbibers) plus metal shelving, an air conditioner and heater.

Carpet leftovers, which had escaped the dumpster at a local furniture store, and a highly uncomfortable wooden office chair, completed the décor. Less-than-comfortable seating, of the more likely the occupant to stay awake theory, proved to be not only logical, but also accurate!

Now, Daddy had a haven…a study hall, if you will. Here, he retreated each evening as soon as he had swallowed a sparse meal. Later, emerging at some post-midnight hour, bleary-eyed and claiming that he was "brain dead," he'd drop onto the first available spot and nap.

After only a few short hours of sleep, he'd shower, grab his books, briefcase and lunch box, and race back to campus and classrooms. A routine, that with very few alterations, he followed for five years. He'd read textbooks out loud to me and when he was too hoarse and/or sleepy to continue, I'd read them out loud to him…punctuating the oral wisdom with, "George, wake up! Pay attention! You have a test tomorrow!"

The team-studying worked…he was on the honor roll each of the eight semesters he was in veterinary school, after being on the President's honor roll the first two semesters he was back at OSU.

However, Autumn, 1968, found neither of us certain that we had EVER made a right decision about anything…in particular veterinary school and adoptions!

Terminal tiredness set in…on our little family…and on our marriage.

By the end of the semester, George was already beginning to show the strain of too many demands on his waking hours. So was I!

We needed to be at least a half-dozen people to keep up with what faced us daily. We were, however, only a young couple, pulled in many directions. We keenly felt the responsibility for our family's present circumstances and George was concerned for the future of his wife and sons. His life evolved into a series of inner struggles that lasted for at least the next ten years. Had we been privileged to gaze into a crystal ball, we would probably have just called a halt to his being in school. Ignorance, however—if not bliss—at least was a blessing.

We edged forward, minutes at a time.

A cloud accompanied George to class…GPA! A high grade point average was crucial to his being allowed to even make application for veterinary school. His first semester back at OSU, his GPA was unbeatable: four point! All A's and the president's honor roll! All of that with the responsibility for a wife and two children…and he was simultaneously taking science courses that were intended to be taken consecutively. (His advisor said, that, had he known what George was doing, he would not have approved such a difficult schedule. The "approval" was done by the advisor's secretary.)

What an accomplishment!

We were excited…and amazed.

The following semester, the spring of 1969, his grades were still extraordinarily high.

Soon after the spring semester got underway, he made application for veterinary school. Our hopes rose that he would be accepted on the first try. We believed that two semesters of top grades averaged into his previous college work would be impressive.

However, as vital as good grades seemed, they weren't the only criteria. We'd been told many times that the proper recommendations from the right people weighed heavily with the admissions committee.

To top it all, we were advised that fully one-third of the committee's consideration concerned the applicant's verbal responses during two personal interviews. George intensely dreaded those interviews.

To us, the odds seemed to not be good. There were more than 600 applicants for the Class of '73 and only forty-eight first-year students would be accepted. We both remained apprehensive. We wondered if lightning needed to strike the committee or some minor miracle should occur for them to accept him into the class. We were plagued with thoughts of hundreds of reasons that might keep him from being accepted, even with the right grades, fine recommendations and correct answers to the committee. Concern was with us every waking minute. If he were not accepted, what would he do? Neither of us was employed and one year back in college with no further degrees wouldn't look good on resumes.

In April 1969, shortly after the committee ceased interviewing, fully three months before the letters of acceptance or rejection were to be mailed to applicants, the phone rang at mid-morning on a Saturday. The caller, identifying himself as a member of the committee, asked to speak to George, who looked thoroughly thunderstruck as he listened.

"I know how much you want to be a member of our incoming class."

"Yes, sir!"

"I, also, know that you have a wife and two very small sons. Because of that, of course you'd appreciate knowing what you will be doing for the next several years."

"Yes, doctor, I would. If I'm not accepted now, rather than reapply to veterinary school, I may apply to graduate school and see what happens with that. I quit a really good job last year and I need some way to provide for my family. I don't think that going back to work for Purina is what either Carolyn or I would like."

"I certainly understand your concern not only for your professional future, but for the future of your family. George, I want you to know that what I'm sharing with you this morning, you cannot tell anyone else, except your wife. Normally, you would find out whether or not you've been accepted into the class when the letter arrives in July. However, it doesn't seem right to leave you hanging until the last minute, not knowing what you'll be doing in August…whether or not you'll be in vet school.

"So, I'm telling you now—CONGRATULATIONS! You're a member of the Class of '73! And, even bigger congratulations are in order. You cannot tell anyone this, now or while you are in school, but out of the more than 600 applicants, George, you were our number one choice!"

Stunned, George said, "Thank you, sir. Thank you very much!"

Grinning, hanging up the phone and grabbing me all in one motion, he yelled, "Can you believe it? We're on our way!"

It seemed that our miracle had just happened!

Innocently, as we celebrated, we had no idea of the price that would be extracted in the coming years.

Concern with school and a professional future began to rearrange George's priorities. Somehow, our young family fell further down the line. It wasn't planned, neither was it desired. It just happened.

Economics of daily living became a large issue, demanding satisfaction from his already-full schedule. Too many claims and not enough hours in the day to fulfill them.

Academics aside, familiar day-to-day necessities became even more important as the money to purchase them decreased in our savings. Forget any luxuries. How to meet our basic needs became an almost unreachable goal. How could we buy groceries, pay utilities and tuition, buy books, gasoline and laundry soap for the never-ending diaper stack...with a double-zero income?

The time required for class work and homework prevented George's getting a job, other than his attending the monthly Army Reserve meetings. His position as a company commander added to his responsibilities and took the last few moments he had to spare. However, the salary was desperately needed, so he juggled things as best he could, to attend meetings.

During the summers between 1969 and 1972, he applied for active duty and we spent time at Fort McClellan, Alabama; Fort Smith, Arkansas; and Fort Benning, Georgia; as a family. Other times, the little boys and I stayed in Stillwater while he went to training sites, helping train young soldiers to fight in the unpopular U.S. involvement in Southeast Asia.

End of summer duty meant that we had a few dollars to keep us going for a while. Also, we could take advantage of the commissary...we'd buy cart-loads of canned goods, boxes, bags and bottles of everything we anticipated needing for the next nine or ten months. Then, we'd pile it in our aging car and pickup and head back to school.

Keeping the family financially afloat was my responsibility, also. We had decided that we didn't want to leave the children with a sitter...it was too expensive and, besides, no one wanted to keep David anyway!

In-between mothering our growing babies, I tried to supplement George's Army Reserves income by typing for college students. At the pathetic rate of fifty cents for each perfectly typed page, I could hardly make payments on the typewriter, much less pay for the typing paper, ribbons and my time. Pre-computer typing was not a lot of fun! Regardless, thousands of pages came through that typewriter during those five years at OSU!

Getting clients wasn't difficult, once the students realized that I not only typed but I also corrected their papers!

Yes, I could not bear to knowingly type poor punctuation, dreadful spelling and bad grammar. Even graduate students were guilty of submitting disgraceful work to me and they were able to turn in papers that appealed to their professors when I finished with them.

While George was in school, I typed for at least thirty other veterinary students per year, in addition to many students in other disciplines. I rather quickly learned to appreciate the medical vocabulary, plus something about diseases, symptoms and diagnoses. It was a valuable education for me, as I later worked full-time in our veterinary hospitals.

Once he was a student in the College of Veterinary Medicine, time for studying became even more of a challenge for George.

First-year students spent an average of forty-eight hours per week *in the classroom.* Saturdays included!

Plus, there was after-class study in anatomy lab (until 11 p.m.). Weekends and holidays gobbled up the hours.

How could a person study, much less remember, material, when he was too tired to exist? For him, words became a gray haze on a white background. Proper preparation for four-hour tests still had to be made, somehow, even when tiredness closed his mind and eyes.

The answer came, in what would be our lifestyle for the four years of vet school: George would study until he could not handle it any longer. As he began to doze, I would stop typing and start reading the textbooks aloud to him.

It didn't take me too long to learn the proper pronunciation of medical terms and I would quiz him, one paragraph at a time, all too frequently until 3:00 a.m.

Soon, it seemed, that we had two veterinary students in our household, with only one paying tuition and getting the degree.

During those weary days and nights, it was no one's fault that the full-time care of our sons became 95% my responsibility. There was, and is, no blame. George simply did not have the time, either to share in or to notice that it happened. It was another fact of our life, one that we accepted, like it or not.

Sometimes, in subsequent encounters over an action of one of our sons, George and I crossed verbal swords. Accusations would fly:

"YOU raised them this way!"

"WELLLLLLLLLLLlllllllllllllllllllllll ! Where were you when they were being raised by me?"

"I was busy trying to prepare a future for all of us!"

"Yeah? Well, guess what? This is that future!"

Parental disputes that might have arisen, no matter what the setting was. No apologies needed.

None made.

CHAPTER FOUR
Less Than Perfect?

It was no wonder that my stringent, self-imposed housekeeping guidelines eventually became unmanageable. Our increasingly small home, inhabited by four energetic people, barely offered breathing space. Daily, I frantically attempted to shove the mushrooming disarray into place. Predictably, it daily oozed out again. Everywhere. Vacated shoes at the front door, toys under the sofa, candy wrappers atop the teeny TV.

Partially dismantled miniature automobiles, abandoned in the narrow hallway, lay in shadows, awaiting the foot of the first unsuspecting adult to send both vehicle and foot speeding out of control.

Nightly, in the sleeplessness that fueled our ever-growing exhaustion, George and I would wonder aloud to each other: "How did our lives reach this point? What can we do to gain control, again, if indeed we ever had been in control?"

Wall-to-wall, twenty-four-hour-a-day lunacy set in!

Books, clothing, furniture. Children, meals, homework. Such a growing volume of possessions. The accumulation of more than six years of marriage, family and school squeezed themselves into our extraordinarily compact home.

Accusations replaced conversation…polite communication, not frequently a long suite in our increasingly volatile personalities, decreased.

George's academic load continued to occupy his life.

Simple survival occupied mine.

My housekeeping standards became roadblocks: They juggled for position, vying with the children's necessary demands for my attention. It made little difference how fast I moved. I was always twenty steps too slow.

Over time, George and I lost the cohesiveness that we should have been building.

Unanswered questions about David multiplied.

Days turned into nightmares.

Our home became a battleground.

As pressures mounted, our lives seemed to fragment.

Decades later, our 20/20 hindsight tells us that the guilt trips we laid on each other individually and on ourselves collectively were the product of our desperate searches for our way out of the maze.

Responsibilities that we should have been sharing became grounds for naming culprits in many situations. If the typing of a homework assignment were not finished until 2:00 a.m., it was because "I couldn't get it typed" because "I didn't get something else finished sooner" because "I had to chase kids" or "fix a meal…" etc.

Sharing and good times faded. Aware of this, we made occasional efforts to undo mutual hurts.

Not always successfully.

Swift solutions to our problems didn't exist. We were going to have to take our lives one day at a time to work things out.

Sound simple?

Not exactly!

Occasionally, in a fit of self-pity, I thought that it seemed harder for me than for George, who, as a middle child was challenged by sibling rivalries and lived to tell about it.

On the other hand, I had grown up as an "only child"…more accurately I was the "ours" in a "yours, mine and ours" situation. I was the only offspring of my parents' marriage and thirteen/twenty-two years younger than their children by their first marriages. I experienced whatever spoiling their limited finances could afford, along with their loving but nearly suffocating protectiveness.

Although my birth date was to have been after the middle of January, as

Mother said, I "blew in with a snowstorm" on November 9th. She often told me, "Your premature arrival probably saved your life. The umbilical cord was knotted around your neck and was strangling you." She always increased the drama of the story, saying that, she turned her face to the wall when she saw how blue my skin was from lack of oxygen and she counted the precious moments slipping past while the doctor worked over me.

When I was a preschooler, I listened with fascination as she recounted the events surrounding my birth on that wintry evening. She told me that when she caught her first glimpse of me, she thought that I was already dead, as no signs of life were apparent.

She didn't want to watch the doctor trying to encourage me to breathe as it seemed hopeless.

Even as she prepared to hear the words that her tiny daughter "didn't make it," she said that she kept praying, asking God to let her baby live.

There were none of the emergency devices and equipment that are available now. A stressed and challenged newborn either lived or died pretty much on its own. And, after all, I was not born in a hospital, but at my parents' home in Frederick, Oklahoma.

Again and again, the doctor attempted, unsuccessfully, to force air into my underdeveloped lungs. Finally, in a desperate attempt, Mother said the doctor declared, "I'll try one last time," giving a hard smack to my behind…and I bleated into life!

Apparently, my resemblance to a skinned rabbit was amazing…I had lots of long black hair, no eyelashes, no eyebrows and was remarkably small.

Each time Mother repeated the story to me, I would listen in wide-eyed silence, gravely awaiting the outcome…as if, one day, that outcome would be different!

Often, there were tears in Mother's eyes and she would brush them aside as she recalled her own emotions during my birth. She would take me on her lap, rock me and tell me how much she loved me…how proud she was of me…how I made her and Daddy so happy.

The story's highlight was invariably when she would tell me how regular baby clothes swallowed me. My birth weight of three and a half pounds wasn't sufficient to fill out the apparel she was preparing for me, so my first wardrobe consisted of hand-me-down *doll clothes!*

When I would hear this, I would stare at the tiny outfits I used for my own little dolls, laughing as I imagined how outrageous it must have been to wear such garments.

Mother had faced a major hurdle, caring for her tiny infant, while managing her own handicap.

Not only did she have an unusually small baby to care for, but also she had only one arm with which to do it. At the age of five, she had lost her right arm in a gun accident. She had given birth to three other children and cared for them, but a premature baby was a different challenge.

Amazingly, in the rather brief years that I knew her, I never heard her complain about the loss of her arm…what many people would consider her "less than perfect" condition.

Instead, she kept an immaculate home, cared for young children to make extra money, raised award-winning flowers which brightened our otherwise minimal surroundings…and, she asked for help with only two things: cutting her fingernails and rolling her hair. I learned very early to do this for her.

As impossible as it sounds, she even sewed clothing for me, using an old treadle Singer machine. Lots of children had homemade clothes, so I didn't feel too unstylish. Years after her death, when I cleaned out the home I had grown up in, I came across a shoebox filled with old newspapers, cut in strange, tiny shapes. I finally figured out that I was looking at the *patterns for baby clothes* that Mother used for me! It wasn't enough that she had to cut out and sew the clothes; she had to make the patterns, too!

Perhaps, the most amazing ability was her talent for *knitting.* Knitting? With only one arm?

Yes, she managed nicely, holding one long metal needle under the stump of her right arm and deftly producing one item after another with her left hand.

She not only made lovely sweaters with complicated designs for me, she also knitted little booties, sweaters and caps for my baby dolls. This seemed such a normal occurrence that in my childish innocence I didn't understand why other adults made such a fuss about it!

She and Daddy made up for their lack of money by giving me abundant love and extravagant affection. I never felt "poor" although I discovered, after I was grown, that we had been pretty low on the financial barometer.

The fact that our home had only linoleum, not carpet, and outdoor plumbing instead of an indoor bathroom…to say nothing of the fact that we had no automobile (we walked in our small hometown, took a bus or train out of town) somehow was not important to me. "Things" and possessions were not as valuable as what was INSIDE of me.

George's financial circumstances as a child were similar: Reared on a farm at Guthrie, Oklahoma, his family had the same sort of outdoor "facilities"…bedraggled vehicles limping on their last puff of gasoline…his father gone for years to the oilfield while he, at about age seven, and his older brother arose early and stayed up late to feed a herd of cows, often turning up late at school in the process. They were, also, kept busy taking care of hogs and chickens, cutting wood every weekend—even in the snow. They quickly became known as "10 o'clock scholars" due to their late arrival time for class.

The family, although white, lived in a predominately black farming neighborhood where the white kids walked to school watching the black youngsters ride on a school bus. George recalls how the black children also were able to participate in the school lunch program while he and other poverty-level white children carried cold fried egg sandwiches for their lunches. The Kendalls skimped along, stretching their pennies and nickels. The mother of the family taught school some of their growing-up years, giving them additional income.

A lack of affectionate displays between family members helped build an emotional wall that was difficult for George to break through when he reached adulthood. "I love you" was not usually part of his family's vocabulary, he told me more than once.

His rather quiet, shy disposition probably was responsible for somewhat of a withdrawal from social and emotional contacts as he grew up. He felt unsure of himself and doubtful that he would be accepted by society-at-large, due to his somewhat deprived childhood.

Any religious input was occasional at best, giving him even less personal stability than he might have had in other circumstances. The most reassurance he received was winning 4-H honors, money and scholarships, where he excelled in many areas.

Somewhere in his younger life, "imperfections" began to loom large. Self-assurance diminished and George dropped out of college briefly, returning to graduate with a business degree shortly before we married.

One hundred eighty degrees in the other direction, my parents had encouraged me and I was a top scholar. Responding to their praise, I appreciated and worked hard at the gift God had given me as a pianist.

This activity was especially important to me, as my mother changed thousands of baby diapers in order to buy my piano and pay for my lessons. By the time I was in fifth and sixth grades, I was playing for Sunday night services at church.

In junior high I accompanied choral groups, vocal and instrumental soloists. By the time I was sixteen, I was a full-time church organist as well as accompanist for a variety of local groups and soloists. Dedicated to school and my music, I was blessed with several musical and academic awards and scholarships.

Music was an extension of my feelings. One-hour before and two-hour after-school practices were not work—they were pleasure. When I sat at the piano, I knew I was a success…no matter what the other circumstances of my life. God had blessed me with an assurance not only of His love and my future with Him, but with the knowledge that whatever was happening externally, I could have peace, internally.

How I was to need that confidence in a few years!

How often I've called on that strength and assurance! Sometimes, I have to search for those feelings, when they aren't spontaneous…and, perhaps, that's been character building for me. And, there have been times when I talked to God, saying, "Do I really need this? I'm probably pretty much of a character, already!"

Even though my parents weren't religious in the traditional sense, they saw to it that I was exposed to Christian churches and doctrines from a very early age. Various neighbors took me to Sunday School and church from the time I was four years old.

Whoever happened to have a car and wanted me around would let me accompany them. This afforded me a rather ecumenical, interesting church background and when I was the age of ten, I found a church that I stayed with until I graduated from high school.

Without realizing it, I gained the tenacity to face frequent life-shattering problems as the values of my parents forged their solid foundation in my life. Face situations, head on, with determination and no backing down, the way that they did.

The death of Mother, several years before George and I married, and then Daddy's death in 1969, left a void that took years for me to come to terms with. I feel that they still live, however, not only in my happy memories, but, also, in their resources and strength that encouraged me.

***

How I desired excellence for myself!

Top grades, talent in music, the kind of youngster I frequently heard other parents remarking about: "My, how I wish my child could/would be like Carolyn."

Negatively, I was overweight and basically shy, often devastated by the cruel taunting of other children in elementary and junior high school. The more I was teased, the harder I attempted to live up to my rather unrealistic expectations.

I felt that I was just as good as everyone else. Why then, was it so hard to maintain self-esteem? As an adult, the more "perfect" I wanted to become, the further I slipped away from my goals. Slowly, I began to feel even more unfulfilled. The more I tried, the less pleased I was with my results.

Worse, by 1969, I was a young wife and mother with a "less-than-perfect" child.

At that point, many doubts began to gnaw at my confidence. Self-doubts became full-blown and I, foolishly, began comparing myself to other young mothers with whom I was acquainted.

More frightening, I compared David with their "wonderful, healthy, bright, talkative, and normal" babies.

Life bogged down for me.

What would people think of me with a child who was a square peg in a round hole? I wasn't mature enough to understand, that it doesn't make any difference what other people think!

A difference, of course, in our lives is made by what *we do,* not by what *someone else might be thinking!*

One hope loomed in my life: Someday all of David's complications would disappear and he would be like the perfectly normal children we encountered each day. Other, more experienced parents could have told me that I was setting an impossible goal, both for my son and for myself.

However, as I kept those thoughts to myself, not even sharing them with George, John and David, no one knew of the horrible aching that was becoming an obsession to make David normal.

No one, that is, except God.

And, at that point, I wasn't really receptive to what He had to say, even when I asked for His help. How dumb is that? Pretty dumb…and sad….

As a result, my depression deepened.

I decided that God had done this to David; therefore, what could He possibly care about any of us!

In my martyred spirit, I felt that He had turned His back on the four of us.

How could He care whether or not our baby conquers these problems? What does He care if I maintain my sanity, or if I grab a gun and blast David and myself into eternity?

Sadly, those thoughts reared their ugly heads on more than one chilling occasion.

Mercifully, God was watching and listening…He saw to it that we didn't have a gun.

Passing years have given a perspective to even the most awful moments we endured. I wonder now how I could have been so blind and so foolish. After all, in spite of what I felt, God did know about our problems and about us.

He DID know.

He DOES know.

And, wonderfully, He does CARE!

All those difficult years, He hurt with us, even when I didn't realize it.

And, He did want to help, even when I couldn't admit it.

In fact, He was The Answer for which we were searching.

We had to come to that simple realization for ourselves.

In our years of blindness, though, we didn't recognize The Answer, so we kept searching.

And waiting.

While He waited for us to come to Him…

He waited…

CHAPTER FIVE
How Much More?

Our version of "The Search for The Answer" was on! In earnest! Days, which had already too quickly turned into weeks and months, were filled with all of the family activities we could handle.

"Student poverty" for us reached such a low level in 1972 that we were actually eating leftover World War II rations, thirty years old, but better than nothing. When George's reserve unit began hauling the pre-packaged meals to the city dump, he asked for approval to appropriate them as they were going to be destroyed, anyway.

For more than six months, we survived by opening, seasoning, heating and praying over the olive-drab, military-colored cans and packages. Occasionally, our stomachs resisted, along with our better senses! Frequently, we were amused by what we'd find in our "surprise" bundles from a war that had ended more than a quarter of a century earlier. Once in a while, rusty cans appalled us. Those were sent, unopened, along with stale food, to the trash.

Every time another military-green can or box was opened, our underlying guilt increased a little. Somehow, we'd just never envisioned ourselves this way. We felt guilty because our finances didn't help our increasingly fruitless search for an answer for David. He was showing little, if any, improvement and a diagnosis kept eluding the doctors.

Also, John's needs were increasing. Little feet needed new shoes. Growing bodies needed larger clothes. Growing minds needed more organized academics…and nothing was free!

It seemed that we had tried at least one of every type of help that was available.

We progressed through the medical community at Stillwater and Enid, Oklahoma, plus the speech and hearing clinic at OSU and the Oklahoma City medical "experts"…the merry-go-round was getting out of hand: attempt to ride one horse and two more replaced it—and none of them could be ridden!

Professionals of all disciplines, accessorized with multiple credentials and years of experience working with "problem children" (as was David's latest classification) examined him…again and again. The common denominator was their answers, which frightened and sometimes horrified us. We were repelled more than once to hear a medical consensus verifying a previous idea that, "Probably, Mrs. Kendall, you are the basic cause of David's problems."

Oh, really? Yes, that was the "diagnosis" when a real diagnosis was beyond the ability of the person making that statement.

Although the cause of David's problems seemed to be more than the capacity of the experts to diagnose, the unified report kept being repeated: "Place the blame on Carolyn!" The thinking might have been: If we blame her, maybe she will take the kid somewhere else!

It was intolerable to me to believe that either George or I had caused his problems. All we had done was to adopt and love him while trying to discover a method to help him. Surely, in all of that, I had not caused the problems. Had I?

No, however, with no definitive diagnosis, there could not be a definitive course of treatment. If no treatment were offered, how could there be a solution?

There was no encouragement from anyone that his condition would ever improve. The only sure thing that the doctors agreed on was that probably everything would deteriorate and turn into more of a nightmare than we already were living.

Looking back, they were right.

And WRONG!

Things in our life were not totally discouraging. John, in the midst of the "terrible twos" and then the "triumphant threes" raced through a seminormal childhood. His life was filled with the daily routines that occupied curiosity-filled hands and minds of pre-schoolers.

Sometimes, we even felt a fleeting hope, such as when David began sitting with support when he reached seven months of age. He noticed music and strangers. As most babies do, he put everything into his mouth. Thankfully, there were occasionally days that were borderline, boringly normal.

There were abundant clues, though, that everything was not as it should be. Often, we simply ignored them, hoping that we were only misinterpreting their significance.

With the wistfulness of a fairy-tale ending, we told ourselves that our story would finish with us all living happily ever after. That wasn't to be—although it remained an inescapable hope.

Signals kept surfacing about something amiss with David. Finally, we could no longer disregard them. Most difficult to understand and the most obvious to observe was the extreme "busy-ness" of David's body.

Awake or asleep, he was seldom without motion even for the briefest time. After he outgrew the bundling, his body seemed to attempt to relax for his much-needed rest times, but his muscles never appeared to cease moving. Arms and legs kept fidgeting even when he was lying down. His limbs and body would twitch, no matter how deeply he was sleeping!

And, when he was awake, he was perpetual motion! It was much more than normal baby activity, curiosity and exploration, for we had experienced lots of that with John. David's actions were a sort of purposeless movement, as though his body were being forced to keep going, propelled by unknown, unidentifiable sources.

An "accident waiting to happen," he watched many items apparently self-destruct at his touch.

Strangely, though, when anything was ruined, the cause never seemed to be from any animosity on his part. No prior planning, no apparent method to the madness. Things just got in his way...or found themselves in his hands where he disposed of them as rapidly and efficiently as he could!

On the other hand, his initials "G.D." for George David, soon took on a new translation: "Garbage Disposal!" He quickly became a diminutive demolition expert before our eyes!

About this time, my housekeeping turned into a relay...and a joke. I couldn't move fast enough to clean up one mess before three more were being unveiled.

When I put John outdoors in the fenced yard, his busy brother (who easily dismantled even the most sturdily constructed projects) accompanied him.

John's howls of protest would send me running to find a wrathful, red-faced older son promising the direst kind of retaliation against his younger brother, for whatever infraction David had committed. No sooner was one encounter calmed, than another would commence. Finally, I often left them to settle their differences "man to man" as my patience grew very thin.

Often, to John's absolute delight, I put David in his highchair, keeping him and everything else safely separated for a few moments. Finally, Big Brother could do some really "important stuff" and not have that little kid interfering with all of it. Additionally, it gave me a small chance to reattempt reorganization of the household.

This move only last briefly...as David soon discovered that a gigantic shove on his tray meant freedom was his! He could be back down, out of the highchair, before I had turned to walk away!

In desperation, I resorted to fastening one of George's belts around him, buckling it in back of the chair seat and leaving him seated and out of action for thirty seconds. Immediately, he would begin *rocking* the chair—back and forth—HARD—screaming at full tilt.

One or two trips to the floor, still fastened in the highchair, didn't make David any smarter about sitting still. I soon found that it was better to set the chair AND the child close to a wall. There, the chair merely bounced off the wall and David, at least, stayed upright. For one or two very short minutes.

Left freely circulating, and to his own devices, the barely-walking David was awesome. Broken dishes, toys hurled the length of the room, divan pillows uprooted and ripped apart...the child had the strength of an adult...and he was only a year old! The intensity with which he wordlessly attacked every object in his path (furniture being no exception) both fascinated and frightened us. There seemed to be no "plan of attack" and there was, and remains, no mean streak in him. The other side of the coin was a complete lack of remorse after he turned something into shambles.

Cause and effect were something that Dave did not understand. What we didn't know then and we have since learned, is that his "not understanding" was perfectly typical of a person with his type of brain damage. It was just one of the pieces of information that no one bothered to tell us...

Consequently, being told "no," or isolated in his room when he was older, was meaningless for him. He didn't connect the crime with the punishment. He regretted the punishment, of course, but didn't know why he was being punished.

At that time, we didn't know that he didn't understand. The circle of "crime and punishment" became very confusing for him, to say nothing of how George and I felt.

Robot-like, David continued to bulldoze through each day. His destructive nature did nothing to endear him, or me for that matter, to our family and friends. Frankly, no one wanted our "little monster" around. And, I honestly couldn't blame them.

Most people with whom we were acquainted appeared to intellectually accept what we told them when we said that we believed David had a brain injury at birth. However, with almost no professional expertise to back up our feelings, people seemed emotionally unable to accept our explanations for his frequently bizarre behavior.

Even the persons closest to us plainly showed that they believed his problems were caused by my failure to make him mind!

Certainly, David's actions must have appeared that way. So little was known or understood about birth-related brain injury in the late '60s and early '70s that people assumed a "naughty" or "different" child must surely have a "bad mother." I tried to understand their reasoning, but many times my nervous system was so saturated with it all, that there was no way I could sort everything out. What I really needed was time to myself. Quiet time…a few minutes to be alone and calm some of my fears…I understood that George needed the same sort of time to be alone…to be away from books and school and studying and have a chance to think of something other than "what do I do next…"

No such luck!

Baby sitters cost money.

Relatives, few in number and even fewer having compassion, were overwhelmed by David's mere presence. They were less willing to keep our son than a stranger would have been. At least that's how they appeared to us—and how they sounded when occasionally we asked for their help.

Most of our friends quietly excused themselves when I desperately appealed to them to keep the children, "just for an hour or so." One friend who didn't was Jaryl Everist, herself the mother of two little girls the ages of our sons. She did look after the boys and I felt like kneeling and kissing her hand any time that she did! Occasionally, another friend or relative might take pity on us and keep the boys for a short while, giving us a brief and very welcome time to regroup.

Twenty-four hours a day of non-stop mothering…no time for anything else. It exhausts me even now to recall it.

George and I kept asking doctors, and ourselves, "Is so much activity 'normal' in one small body?" John had done all of the "right" and "normal" things—even ahead of Dr. Spock's timetable. And, if John were normal, then what in the world was David? Who had the problem? Was it David, or was it us? Or, as the experts kept repeating, simply a case of "something wrong with Carolyn." Could it be that I was not capable of being a good mother? Was I doing something to keep David continually agitated?

Why couldn't he be STILL?

He was two years old and not beginning to form sounds that made any sense. Was that my fault, too? Why was he so obviously left-handed that he seldom used his right arm and hand? Was that, too, my fault? Why was he so awkward? Always stumbling and falling, careening into walls, furniture and toys...

Was the drug that had been prescribed for his hyperactivity when he was only fifteen months old part of the problem?

Lots of questions.

Few answers.

There was, however, one distinct truth: As David became increasingly active, I became increasingly vocal!

Although my family will shake a collective head in disagreement, I often reminded them that B.C. (Before Children) I did not raise my voice just to make a point. In fact, shining my halo, I let them know that I almost never yelled in any situation. However, by the time the children approached one and three years of age, my lungs were in wonderful shape!

My non-stop admonitions frustrated my family: "Stop!" "Don't drop that!" "Sit down!" etc., etc.

From wake up until go to sleep...time-out only for a deep breath to read stories to the boys, play some games and to enjoy our children's songs as they vocalized along with "Winnie the Pooh" records while George nodded approval.

Then, back to business as usual.

Punishing David was pointless. Whatever disaster happened, it never appeared to be the result of thoughtful planning on his part. Planning aside, he was frequently on the receiving end, literally, when justice was meted out.

Often, he was more amazed than anyone to discover that he was the culprit! He seemed horrified to find that his actions had such non-productive results, except for justice.

From his point of view, he frequently was the victim. An expression of utter disbelief would cross his puzzled face as he realized that HE was the cause…he was not just the innocent bystander. What a surprise for him!

At first, I thought that he had mastered the put-on to cover his own actions. Gradually, I learned that he, truly, didn't view his actions as harmful. To him they were merely happenstance.

John, by now a joyous three-year-old, manfully tried to accept all of the hassles in the household. Our home was full of disruptions and disappointments, however, for him.

Although he was growing up, had been potty-trained for a year and seemed to be a mature little fellow, shortly before his third birthday, his training regressed. I wasn't surprised. In fact, I had half-expected him to return to the predictable babyish behavior after David was born. When he didn't immediately, we congratulated ourselves for having such a well-adjusted child. We could have saved ourselves the kudos!

When David was seven months old and John was almost three, I took the boys from Stillwater to Frederick, Oklahoma, for several weeks while I looked after my aging father, who had recently been diagnosed with prostate cancer. Caring for him seemed to me to be a natural thing to do, since I was the only one of his five children who had taken care of him since my mother's death.

George and I had tried to spend as much time with Daddy as we could. We had called and written to him several times a week, even though long distance phone calls were another strain on our steadily decreasing budget and cell phones with unlimited calling were far in the future.

Before his illness, Daddy still went to work daily, staving off the inevitable retirement that he knew was not far in the future. As long as he had his job in the water and electric plant and a familiar routine, he felt that he had a reason to live. Unfortunately, the cancer diagnosis and his boss' ultimatum for retirement arrived in his life at the same time. They mutually took a toll.

From Thanksgiving 1968, the last time we had seen him, until the April 1969 trip, Daddy had deteriorated shockingly. At the time of David's birth in September 1968, he had appeared his usual cheerful self, looking extremely healthy, considering his mid-seventies age.

At Thanksgiving, there had been a dramatic weight loss, accompanied by an odd yellow cast to his eyes and skin. Ominous feelings had clouded our holiday trip when Daddy announced that his retirement date was to be the following first of July. That news, accompanied by his appearance, forced us to face the fact that he was very ill…probably physically sick due to the impending closing of his work life.

We had tried our best to keep tabs on him, but from 200 miles away, it wasn't possible to do it well. By the time of spring break in April, we knew that the family doctor wasn't doing anything to make a diagnosis or a difference in his plummeting health. When questioned, Daddy still protested that he was "feeling O.K."

Angry at the apparent lack of medical attention and frightened by his symptoms, I recalled that the same doctor had been Mother's attending physician when she died of cancer. I took him to other doctors for their opinions. Finally, following several surgeries, the prognosis was bleak.

Our hearts were heavy and we tried to adjust our family's life so that I could be with him as much as possible. His other daughters and sons showed little interest in caring for him, although all of them had grown children and didn't have the responsibilities that I had.

While the boys and I were with Daddy, several weeks at a time, John became distressed with the upset in his usual circumstances. He saw my attention being further divided. He began sucking his thumb, bed-wetting became routine and both children began to clamor for additional attention. Of course, I knew that they needed reassurance…I needed some, myself!

Eventually, the day came when a decision had to be made…and it was done with an overwhelming sadness that I felt for a long time.

As I had done previously, I pleaded with my two half-sisters to help with Daddy's care and they grudgingly said that they would "look after him." By this time he was almost completely bedfast and required more care than one person alone could do, especially caring for two young children at the same time.

The picture I made of Daddy the morning the boys and I left is poignant. I had always carried a camera and made pictures of all of us every time we were together. I knew this would be the last one.

Trying to be strong, standing outside of my childhood home, Daddy was supported by two of his other children. In the color photo, the hideous yellow tinge is splashed across his skin. He would live less than three more months, but he was still smiling for John, David and me.

I can still hear his last words to me, "Honey, don't worry. You've done all that you can. I know that George and the boys need you. I love you."

And my words to him, "You know I don't want to go…you know that we love you…and we'll see you again."

He had made the grandest effort to please me. He suggested that he go out into the front yard where I had so frequently photographed his smiling face. In his robe and slippers, so thin that I hardly recognized him, his face drawn...dying...yet there he stood, bravely smiling for his baby's final picture of him!

His other daughters took him, against his wishes, to their homes in the Texas Panhandle, saying, "It will be so much more convenient for us for him to be here. That way we won't have to go to his house." In reality, they didn't concern themselves with caring for him at home, but put him in a hospital.

Early on the morning of July 15, 1969, while we were at George's Army Reserves summer duty at Fort McClellan Alabama, the call came...from the husband of one of my half-sisters. It was over.

At least it was over for Daddy. He had died, alone, in the hospital at Amarillo, Texas.

The last four weeks that John, David and I spent in Frederick had claimed a part of our lives that surprised us with its dimension. Suddenly, *everything* seemed unstable. Daddy's cruel illness and death, John's babyishness and David's incredible actions strained every fiber of my being.

"Wonder what's gonna jump up and slap us, next," became one of our more frequent topics.

Quite a lot, as a matter of fact!

CHAPTER SIX
More Questions, No Answers

A filing cabinet drawer is filled with the history I've kept of our children. Each page of notes brings special memories, some wonderful and a few of them disheartening.

Reconstructing the years of discovery and the pain that frequently accompanied them was unimaginably difficult, even considering the available documents. The hardest part seemed to be keeping myself from dawdling over them.

By fifteen months of age, David was becoming more puzzling than ever. At the same time, at the age of three, John was continuing his development into a brighter-than-usual child (not just my assessment, but that of other people) with an insatiable curiosity.

Thoughts I entertained about taking a job to help with our finances vanished as the baby's problems gained momentum. The children needed me at home, and our lack of money couldn't compete with their needs.

Occasionally, I would feel that I was another "Joan of Arc"...although the way that her problems were ended certainly didn't appeal to me!

Although our financial situation in September 1968 had seemed bleak, it was nothing compared to what it would become before May 1973 and graduation. During the same five years, David became increasingly impossible for us to understand.

Our pilgrimages to offices of MDs, psychiatrists, psychologists, speech therapists, etc., usually ended with predictable sameness: their lack of knowledge equaled no help for David. It occurred to us that we either were looking in the wrong places or there really were no answers.

Our road became rockier.

David's hyperactivity drained not only him, but also the other three of us. From the continual motion in his bed and high chair to the really razzle-dazzle stuff of hurling lamps and chairs across open and occupied spaces, we never knew what would happen next. Neither did David!

As David reached his second summer, more conclusions became obvious: Diagnosis and treatment might remain out of our reach. The medical community that we continued to consult appeared to neither care about a cause nor a cure for his various problems.

Fortunately, we were finally pointed in the direction of Dr. William Simon at Enid, Oklahoma. Dr. Simon, an outstanding, caring pediatrician, as well as a wonderfully patient, understanding man, probably saved our lives.

After making an initial exam of seventeen-month-old David, Dr. Simon agreed that he was, indeed, hyperactive and brain-damaged. Although the cause remained unknown, the doctor suggested that there might be chemical help available. Not a wonderful answer, but it might provide some assistance.

At this point, if there were no help for David with medications, maybe the doctor would like to prescribe some for me! Not really, but in my exhausted state, the idea did seem appealing.

Dr. Simon explained that finding a drug to help David would be, at best, a rather "hunt and peck" approach. Even so tentative a statement provided more hope than we had previously been given.

After seventeen months of searching, perhaps we were going to find some kind of help. We proceeded to give our son first one drug, Ritalin, and then later another (Vistaril), followed by yet another. None was helpful.

This was prior to the days of "Attention Deficit Disorder" diagnoses that were popular in the 1980s and 1990s. It was before Ritalin was handed out like candy to help corral revved-up children in classrooms. In 1970 it was a somewhat innovative approach to handling a youngster like David who would swing from a chandelier if he could get to the ceiling!

Dr. Simon explained that in the case of each drug, "Each is a stimulant, which normally has a non-stimulating effect in many hyper children." He went on to say, "These drugs often are able to tranquilize excessively active young bodies rather than 'zipping them up' as happens when the same drug is given to an adult."

We tried.

For several months.

With disastrous results.

We started giving Ritalin to David while we were at Ft. Chaffee, Arkansas, for George's Army Reserve duty. Anyone who has ever been to Ft. Chaffee in July knows the weather, mildly stated, is miserable. Hot, humid and trying on the hardiest of spirits. As if the weather weren't enough, the four of us were confined in the bachelor officers' quarters. The BOQ housing was exactly what the name implied: intended for adults and NOT for families.

Consequently, our two rooms, and a minimally furnished kitchen, contained even less-than-adequate sleeping arrangements. Our two not-quite-half-beds and a chaise lounge were not our idea of comfort.

George and I slept on the uncomfortable (putting it mildly) beds and John claimed the chaise. Our growing David overwhelmed the portable crib. However, it was better to share these surroundings and their unique arrangements than to be separated for most of the summer.

One of my most quoted sayings is, "In every situation there is something good." In this situation, the "good" thing was the price: Cheap!

In these surroundings, we started the Ritalin doses.

Bad news! Very bad.

Rather than calming our over-active child, the medication sent him into even more radical behavior. His body was so hyped up, so "in motion," that we were tempted to sit on him just to keep him in one place for a second or two. Our energies were collectively drained. I verged on hysteria most of the time…just watching our son, who was absolutely unable to stop moving.

His little body, even when he was finally asleep, relentlessly moved as it had when he was a newborn. Fingers wiggled, legs kicked, his head tossed in all directions.

Three days of staying close to his crib at naptime finally shoved us in a new direction. It was unnerving as we watched his body's contortions, every limb seeming to be moving simultaneously in numerous different directions.

The sticky summertime weather and lack of air conditioning didn't help any of us to rest, but David suffered the most. Although he had dark circles under his eyes from lack of sleep—and so did the rest of us—he could not be still long enough to get any rest.

"George, would you watch this?" I asked our weary student/soldier. He was trying to find a comfortable position on the smaller-than-life bed. Curious, he looked, then sat up as he saw me placing my hands on David's torso. I had decided that if I held David in place for a few minutes, then he'd surely drop off to sleep, the way he did when he was "bundled." Perhaps the other three of us could then have a few quiet moments.

"What're you doing? Is this going to help? Sure wish something would give us a few minutes of rest," he commented, tiredly walking across the bare wooden floor. He stood at my side.

"Look at this! Would you believe it? No matter what I do, he won't quit moving!"

My hands were lightly forcing David's chest and abdomen to stay in one place, but I couldn't believe my eyes: His arms and legs were still thrashing about!

"Let me help. Maybe if I hold his arms and legs, then he'll go to sleep," George offered.

With my husband hanging on to our baby's arms with one hand and legs with his other hand, and with me holding down the rest of his body, we were shocked to discover that his feet were still in motion!

"Good grief! He looks something in the movies…someone who's possessed!"

That conclusion occurred to us each at the same time and we had to smile, as we said it in unison. Fascinated, we continued to watch the performance.

I slid my hand from David's thighs to his ankles and then down to his feet. We were thunderstruck as we watched his toes continue beating out a rhythm to an unheard drummer!

Puzzled, we wondered out loud, "What next?"

Ritalin obviously was not going to be helpful.

Looking through the yellow pages, I came across the number in Ft. Smith for Holt-Krock Clinic. The ad at least sounded hopeful. In desperation, I called and tried to briefly explain our problem.

"We can make an appointment for David to have an EEG," I was told, "after the clinic contacts Dr. Simon for his recommendations and permission."

O.K., here we were, several hundred miles from home and in unfamiliar professional hands…again. We hoped that an EEG would give us some clues to the cause of David's increasing hyperactivity. His increasing misery made us feel helpless. And, if we felt so badly, we couldn't imagine how David must feel!

"Test Day" arrived.

At the huge clinic, I had the usual waiting-room workout with David. Before he became more out-of-control than usual, we were ushered into an exam room.

A nurse attached electrodes to David's scalp while he protested violently. His responses were full of energy and lung power. Everyone within earshot knew that something was taking place! It was an understatement to say that he was going to be "intolerant' of the situation.

Anyone who has had an EEG knows that the patient must be quiet so that the brain wave recordings are accurate.

No such luck!

Dr. Simon had suggested to the Holt-Krock staff, and had given permission, for a tranquilizer for David during the testing, "if he needs it."

"Needs it? David? Give one to me and another to his mother," the nurse commented. "Perhaps we can get finished with this while we are still alive and sane."

We hoped that a tranquilizer would bring relative calmness—relative, that is, as a thunderstorm is to a tornado. In reality, nothing short of total unconsciousness would have slowed him.

At last, in an effort to get some sort of evaluation, the nurse handed the protesting child to me. There we were in the testing chair, David and I, electrodes and all. Fruitlessly, I attempted to keep him still.

He invented new ways to grab the electrodes. He carried on his version of a conversation, jabbering at everything in the room.

Eventually, the tranquilizer began to bring a few peaceful moments just about the time that the nurse and I were ready to give up.

A general anesthesia could not be considered, as it would have altered the test results. The technician took advantage of the brief calm and the recordings were complete.

The results, we were told, were eventually read by a "well-qualified, highly proclaimed specialist in St. Louis—nothing abnormal.'"

Easy for that person to say!

Surely, somehow, somewhere, someone had an answer for us.

The question remained: Where?

CHAPTER SEVEN
A Glimmer of Hope

Exit Ritalin.

Enter Vistaril.

Same results.

David's seemingly limitless supply of energy appeared to actually increase with each succeeding drug.

Dr. Simon was puzzled. As he said, "David is a classic case. He should have responded favorably to this treatment."

"Classic" or not, I felt some shreds of my civility and sanity slipping out of sight. Our son's symptoms were getting worse, if that were possible.

Communication between George and me was becoming even more difficult. Friends and relatives continued to be of minimal help. How could anyone be helpful when even the experts seemed to be so lacking in diagnoses and treatments?

John observed our deteriorating family and demanded more attention. It appeared that he felt that his security was being threatened, and as a helpless four-year-old he couldn't handle it.

To try to give John a chance to be with his peers, and provide a more normal atmosphere for him, we enrolled him in play school five days a week. This gave him necessary time with other youngsters.

He learned more about interacting with children who did not have the multiple problems of his little brother and it gave David some occasion for my undivided attention.

I welcomed the change of pace, as it meant there would be a couple of hours a day when there were fewer "mothering" demands for me to face.

Shortly after David's second birthday, we abandoned Dr. Simon's third prescription recommendation. We started anxiously on the fourth one.

"Maybe this one, Mellaril, will be helpful," we once again hoped. We crossed our fingers and prayed.

After three ineffective drugs, there was one that helped!

Mellaril was the answer for the next *seven years.* David was started on ten milligrams, three times daily, which was the usual beginning dosage for an institutionalized adult. David was still a baby, only twenty-four months old!

The high dosage actually worked!

The liquid medication must have tasted even worse than it smelled, which was saying quite a lot. Consequently, morning, noon and night (after fasting from liquids so that he'd be thirsty enough to drink the concoction) I coaxed, pleaded, threatened, hollered at and promised…just to get the foul tasting liquid down David's throat.

When it was mixed with chocolate syrup, David's favorite flavor, and milk, to mask the terrible taste, we could get the medicine in his mouth. While swallowing might NOT be the next step, taking it "straight" was impossible.

The calming effect was remarkable, almost from the first dose. David was, at last, able to sit still for a few minutes.

He would, at least, look at the pages of a book before tossing it aside in sixty seconds. Television, the national electronic babysitter, began to capture his attention for a moment or two.

Dave would listen to a hasty, abbreviated version of a childhood tale, or to a song, while sitting on my lap. For the first time, he would actually play with a toy for a brief time…before wandering off to another activity. Although he was still far too active, we felt that a significant milestone had been reached. To parents who have only "normally active" pre-schoolers, the meager amount of peace we experienced with his slowing down can neither be explained nor understood.

Over the years, we encountered many youngsters in our home, veterinary hospital and church. Also, we've known many others through our teaching two-year-olds in Sunday school. Some of them occasionally were labeled as "hyper," usually by their tired parents. We never saw one who even approached the extraordinary busy-ness of David at that age.

Those occasional times when David would be a bit quieter gave us encouragement. Maybe, we were on the right track, at last.

He began sleeping without his body moving all of the time. His attention span improved slightly.

Today, to meet and observe David, it hardly seems possible that hyperactivity ruled his childhood.

As years passed, David spent hours silently studying, working on a vast collection of his architectural drawings, constructing intricate model villages, playing with the computer or just absorbing hundreds of ideas and information from the library at home and school. Thankfully, he eventually did all of it without chemical intervention, although the metamorphosis took long and frequently harrowing years.

While he was taking the Mellaril, the dosage was increased regularly as his body required more of it to maintain a level helpful for him. The result was better self-control and selection of activities. In short, for him to approach more age-appropriate behavior and attention span, more medication was required. We didn't like it, but that was the reality of the situation.

In 1970, as he was enjoying his calmer existence, another problem loomed on our horizon: He was two years old and should have been making intelligible sounds. At the very least, he should have made the "m" and a few other sounds that are pre-requisite to speaking the English language. Also, he should have been peddling a tricycle, walking up and down stairs with alternating feet, all of which we later learned are required for speech patterns.

He could do none of it.

Nothing, no sound, that he uttered, made the slightest sense.

It seemed that he knew what he wanted to articulate…and he tried very convincingly to make sensible sounds…but they came out all wrong. It appeared to George and me that the message going from his ears, through his brain and out his mouth was being garbled somewhere.

What he actually said bore no resemblance to what he should have said or to what we thought he wanted to say. Rather, a strange assortment of mismatched vowels and consonants poured out. Creative guessing games occupied his attempts to make himself understood, with one or another of us pointing out items or making suggestions about what WE thought HE was saying.

What next?

Speech therapy!

We felt that Someone was looking out for us. In Stillwater, at OSU, there was an outstanding speech and hearing clinic…just what David needed. Imagine that!

Thank You, God!

College students, majoring in speech and hearing education, served as apprentice clinicians. They were given academic credit and experience while working with patients of all ages and requirements. There were clients who suffered speech deficiencies from strokes or other trauma, as well as from birth defects.

A wealth of experience was provided to the college students, at no cost to them. They broadened their horizons while providing desperately needed clinical care for the patients.

Of course, therapy does cost money. We were too "financially challenged" to pay for the work they would be doing with David. Bless the March of Dimes! That organization donated tuition money for three years to enable David to begin to learn to speak.

When he started therapy, I took him twice weekly to the huge, red brick building on campus. That was not as easy as it sounds…Just getting David into the place was a spectator sport! He would be kicking and screaming as we'd make our rather dramatic entrance. The collegians and professors must have come to dread the sight of the mini-skirted, 117-pound mother, literally dragging her thirty-five-pound son up the sidewalk and into the waiting room.

The show was on, twice a week!

Once inside the building, the ballyhoo didn't end! More darting by David, under, around and behind furniture, hollering while trying to avoid the groups of arms that swooped his way, as students tried to grab him. When a lucky person clamped down on him, he would literally be hauled off to a therapy room.

Many hours, I sat outside those rooms, looking through the one-way glass, tears silently rolling down my face. David, in full view, would be trying to avoid being helped! He'd jump, run, squirm, jabber and sulk, generally driving the young student-teachers sideways!

Capturing his attention took a minor miracle, even though he'd had his Mellaril a couple of hours earlier. A last-ditch effort would come in the threat of punishment, but before the sixty-minute, seemingly day-long, hour was over, he would wear down enough to pay a small amount of attention to the instructor.

At home, George, John and I worked with him, also.

"Homework" was unpleasant for David, as he didn't know why he was forced to do all of the mouth exercises. He couldn't understand why we would go over and over and over such things as putting his tongue in a particular place in his mouth while attempting to force a funny-sounding "hiss" out through his lips.

And, if things were unpleasant at home, they could be much worse at therapy!

"He's here, again. That kid nobody can work with!"

Apprehension built each time we parked and got out of the car. I visualized our movements being monitored as we approached the building. I felt I could read their minds as we started up the sidewalk.

On several previous occasions, I'd overheard unkind comments and dreaded the scenes. It was difficult to hear the remarks of the students, but I could understand how they felt. Matter of fact, for years I dreamed about it, recalling my defensive feelings as David and I hurtled through the narrow front doors. The receptionist would fix a grim smile and tell us to wait a few moments.

Few *moments*? It was an eternity every Tuesday and Thursday!

At that point, the chase was on! Of course, it was hard on David, as Mellaril only went so far in calming him. It was equally hard on the student-teachers, as they wanted to *teach*, not *chase* our rambunctious child for an hour.

It was equally difficult for me, to quietly observe what he was doing during therapy. I could not go in after him and put a stop to all of it. Instinctively, I knew that if I "rescued" the teachers and the lunging, screaming child even once, his chance for improvement might, also, be gone. Maybe forever.

I understood that the teachers had to establish their authority with him. He had to learn to trust them and to pay attention to them. I could not, would not, interfere.

Days evolved into weeks and then into months.

Slowly, he calmed, responding to simple bribes at first: It was obvious by his size that he loved to eat. After a few weeks of exercise chasing David, the resourceful young teachers pounced on this, amply fortifying themselves before each session with snacks for him. They managed to capture his attention through his palate. Cheerios and M&Ms candies were the attention-getters the instructors needed.

The ability to articulate properly formed speech patterns involved more than George and I ever imagined. We learned, however.

People who are blessed with spontaneous, easily understood speech patterns are, indeed, fortunate. David just was not that lucky. Every sound and syllable that he eventually was able to say had to be structured and exercised.

Speaking did not come naturally. Patience, ingenuity and fifteen years of therapy went into the almost-perfect speech patterns that David enjoys today. People who don't know his history find it difficult to believe that this gregarious man had difficulty with speech.

He was in therapy twice, then three times, then five times weekly, continuing until the end of his junior year in high school.

The first positive results came almost three months after David's therapy sessions started. Shortly before Christmas 1970, for no known reason, David delegated his most winning smile to me, opened his mouth, and startled me with the greeting, "Hi, Guy!"

Not exactly the traditional first words—"Mommy" or "Daddy," which parents usually expect!

Nevertheless, we were thrilled! These first understandable words, blurted out as the lights of our Christmas tree illuminated our son's face, seemed a Christmas miracle, indeed!

He was twenty-seven months old...and, finally, our child could say something that someone other than himself could understand!

Hallelujah!

Our excitement paled beside what David appeared to be feeling, for he kept repeating the phrase, savoring the feel, as well as the sound of it. Verbal communication, vital to interpersonal relationships and to our individual sense of well-being, was now David's!

Unlike fairy tales, though, things did not move along "happily ever after" from this point. Our wrestling matches continued en route to speech therapy...tears and uncooperativeness dimmed only slightly for David...however, he had taken a step up his difficult mountain of disabilities.

"God, are you pushing...or shoving?" I frequently directed this question, along with countless others, to the Author and Giver of Life. In our haste to help David conquer his problems, along with our unanswered questions, we monotonously renewed our requests to God: "Make David well." "Help him to be normal" (whatever that means—in our case it translated: "Less troublesome, embarrassing and time-consuming for us")."Help us find someone to assist him, and us."

No quick-fix was in sight.

No drive up-drive off answers.

In a society where instant component parts could be readily made into a perfect whole, limitlessly reproducing a matrix , it seemed unthinkable that this child couldn't be "fixed up" or made "almost perfect." We *wished* that he could be quietly slipped into the mainstream unnoticed and unnoticeable.

"What are You trying to prove, either to us or with us…Do you even HEAR me, God?"

Always another question. Another answer needed.

No, the Heavens didn't open up and booming voices provide the immediate answers we wanted to hear. Instead, time ticked along.

When David was two and a half, we knew that we needed additional help outside of the therapists and ourselves. Medically, it didn't seem available. Comfort and assistance from relatives seemed evasive. Nominal help in extreme circumstances came from a few loyal, long-suffering friends.

Plainly, few people we knew seemed to have any answers. At least, no one in our small area of Earth. George and I agonized, trying to find answers. Sometimes, we fought with each other while doggedly continuing our search.

Looking back, it seems both humorous and melancholy that in our youth and desperation, my husband and I actually believed that *one, single* answer would suffice for all of David's many problems…and ours.

Sometimes, adults can have, left over from their childhoods, a kind of babyish, selfish consciousness, demanding that problems be solved swiftly and with finality…a kind of "git 'r done" mentality. Dispose of mistakes and injustices of life…get on with living! How easy it was, to ask that our prayers receive the *exact* answer that we desired. That attitude was alive and well within us.

It became one of our own worst stumbling blocks.

We believed that we'd often been ignored, not only by our Creator, but also by members of the medical and educational communities.

Worse, we felt as if we'd sometimes been given *negative* answers from God. "No. Sorry, Kendalls. You cannot receive another 'perfect child.' After all, you already have John, who's bright and fun and not a lot of trouble. Concentrate on him. What more could you possibly want?"

Or, "Why can't you two just admit that your second son isn't normal now and never will be?"

It's not a good idea to put words in God's mouth!

In time, those feelings, contradictory to everything that we wanted to feel about David, overtook us. Depression hung around…to an astonishing degree. It found a comfort zone, lingering lazily in our lives for several years, cropping up at unexpected, unwelcome moments.

Disastrous consequences awaited our children and us if we didn't change. The more frustrated that I became, the more unstable I was…and the more unable I found myself to cope with even the smallest details of daily life.

I shrieked and screamed, hollered, threatened and punished. Then, guilt trips would start the whole ridiculous process all over again.

A frightening merry-go-round was forming in our lives. One crisis led to another.

George wasn't left out. The long hours in the classroom at veterinary school shortened his temper. He would leave for class early each morning, so tired from a night of studying that he could hardly find the school parking lot. He returned as much as twelve to fourteen hours later, with every ounce of physical and mental strength eroded.

The weekends that he attended Reserve meetings claimed precious hours that he could have spent writing term papers or studying for four-hour exams. Still, he had his family to support and the military commitment was the only way that he could do it.

John, David and I each suffered, when "Daddy got behind on lessons." Grades were everything. In veterinary school, no grade below a "C" was recorded on a transcript. If a student made less than a "C" in any class, there was no chance to re-take the class, working for a better grade. Every member of the class proceeded through the same classes on the same schedule and graduated together.

Low grades would mean that a student had to have enough "A's" the following semester, during which time he or she was on academic probation, so that the low grade could be averaged in, for at least a "C" grade. If not, the student was out of veterinary school, for good.

Although George's grades were so good that he made the honor roll every semester, he never stopped worrying. The students faced critical tests almost daily and always several each week. Chronic crises set in.

The pressure mounted for him, as a husband, father and student. Of course, he began to react to it. Soon, all of us shared in his impatience.

It is to their credit that neither John nor David ran away from home! They are still loving, caring, wonderful sons. During the hectic five years at OSU, they exhibited patience and understanding far beyond what could have been expected during times when each of us was barely able to deal with our circumstances.

We are deeply grateful for their love and acceptance of us as parents, for their support of us and sharing of their triumphs and tragedies with us when they were teenagers and now as grown men...for their trust in us.

As parents, we acted childishly in many situations, persistently insisting on our own way and our own terms, especially when we believed that we'd been ignored by God—or worse, when we thought that He was giving us negative answers.

After several years of batting our heads against unyielding walls of self-doubt, we began to listen rather than to make demands of God. We were astounded at what we heard: We had already received An Answer...we simply did not recognize it!

Not that we liked The Answer when we finally acknowledged it. As outrageous as it sounds, we even began to ignore it. The reason? Because it hurt! Our silly pride, feelings, dignity and family relationships all suffered because The Answer was, and is: David's problems are not going to disappear.

The Answer was, and is: We will be given the strength not only to endure but to overcome his problems and the multitude of disruptions that we had, individually and as a family unit.

"No temptation (in this case, temptation to do away with our home, our marriage, our family) has overtaken you but such is common to man; and God is faithful, who will not allow you to be tempted beyond what you are able, but *with the temptation will provide the way of escape* also, that you may be able to endure it."
1 Cor.10:13, New American Standard. The italics are those of this author.

The Bible teaches that, there is no problem, however great, that can overwhelm us, when we trust in God and stay on the path that He has for us. God will give us the strength to meet and overcome any challenge!

In 1971, as this revelation began to dawn on us, we wondered how we could have been so obtuse. We had *assumed* (a dangerous situation) that God neither knew nor cared about our day-to-day-needs.

Honestly, how could we have been so blind?

God knew of our pain, disappointments and searching.

It wasn't that we had been looking in the wrong places for The Answer. We had been looking for the answer that we wanted to hear! We had closed our minds and hearts to what was being told to us, over and over.

Of course, David's problems were not the only ones in our lives. We were much the same as many other families who frequently faced difficult decisions. How nice, if our problems would just disappear. However, the really tough issues of life don't evaporate and we had to come to terms with that truth.

Without those issues, we'd have had very little spiritual or emotional growth. We began accepting the fact, that, there will always be confrontations and difficulties.

Nevertheless, our family was, and is, convinced that, like the phoenix, something beautiful and spectacular *could* rise from the rubble and ashes where we often found ourselves.

St. Francis of Assisi was very wise in his prayer, "God, give us the faith to accept the things we cannot change."

Although we would not be able to change David's problems, we realized that we could change our attitude from rebellion to acceptance. If a circumstance cannot be changed by *outside* intervention, no matter how it is applied (and if it is necessary that some kind of change must occur in order for the problem to be dealt with) then change has to take place *inside* of people.

There might have been no outward, noticeable transformation. Rather, there began a kind of mutation in our spirit.

"Lord, please don't get out of patience with us in this process. Show us how to change and what to do," we prayed.

Miraculously, some transformation did begin, as did a measure of healing.

CHAPTER EIGHT
Taming the Whirlwind

As if life were not already busy enough, during David's first year of speech therapy he, also, began attending the "Exceptional Child Clinic" at OSU. The non-profit classes for pre-schoolers provided a learning experience—free of charge—to Stillwater youngsters who were exceptional physically, mentally and/or emotionally. It was one of the few peer groups offered during the early '70s. David was accepted shortly after I accidentally discovered the existence of the school.

An article in the local newspaper led me to the church building whose facilities were utilized for the needful children. Previously, I had asked numerous people in the area if there were an academic setting for children who were not functioning normally.

No one I talked to knew of any place where these children could get the critical early assistance that was necessary for them to survive in a "normal" world. We had tried another one, without success.

As it turned out, David loved the teachers and the other children. He benefitted from the nearly one-on-one teacher-student ratio.

At that point, he and I began to experience a "revolving-door" syndrome.

Every morning I took John to nursery school, David to therapy followed by his trip to the Exceptional Child Clinic.

Shortly, I retraced my steps retrieving our boys.

Afternoons were busy as we helped David practice his speech therapy while John perfected new skills in crafts and school readiness. I tried to find a couple of hours to type for money.

Nap times, infrequent and punctuated with the boys' requests for story times and glasses of water, ended with no naps for them, while I craved one! The children usually stayed up all afternoon. Underfoot and talkative.

I clearly recall one afternoon when the boys were sitting underneath the kitchen bar that separated the living room and kitchen areas of the trailer. Not wanting to share, they had started to bicker over a couple of toys.

I was arbitrating their disagreement from my vantage point in the kitchen. They were behind the solid wall of the bar, so I couldn't see them. Their increasing fuss caused a commensurate increase in the volume of my voice. Increasing, that is, until I overheard John's stage-whisper to his brother, "Just a second, Dave, and she'll really be yelling!"

I couldn't keep from laughing, seeing how easily I had been drawn into their juvenile net! They knew exactly how I was going to react to their actions…which was a great deal more than even I realized.

The Exceptional Child Clinic gave David a new measure of confidence. We felt that we might at least be getting a start in our search for help.

David's smiling face, shining in a group picture of his 1971 "exceptional class," confirmed that he was the only child in the group who appeared *physically* normal. The remainder of the youngsters formed a mixture of Down Syndrome and obvious physical problems, which branded each as "different."

Every time I left David at class, I thanked God that, "at least he looked alright." Blond hair, blue eyes and always a big smile for everyone. That description perfectly fit David *and* John.

The pre-school that David previously attended was not as successful as this one.

In the summer of 1970 I had received a call from the dean of the School of Home Economics at Oklahoma State. She said that she was so excited to let me know that David had been accepted as a student in the Family Relations and Child Development nursery school. Little did she suspect what a controversy he would cause!

Just being accepted into this prestigious school was a Big Step for any Stillwater family. Most parents, more knowledgeable than we, made application for their offspring at the time of the child's birth! David had been over a year old when we applied. We felt fortunate that he had been considered, much less accepted.

The dean's enthusiasm dimmed somewhat, when I reminded her that David had "a few problems." I had been honest when I completed the application form and she assured me that "it would be good for the student-teachers to have a child who's a challenge."

Really!?

Due to his "exceptional behavior in relation to his peers" (translated: "The other kids hate him when he dumps buckets of water over their heads and gives them the bucket for a hat") David attended the nursery school on a very limited schedule. That was done in order for him to spend as little time with his classmates as possible. It helped the university to maintain a clear conscience in charging the high tuition for him! After all, he was enrolled and attending!

Although we did pay for him to attend class five one-half days a week, the dean generously reduced our fee to one-half when she decided to let David attend only two hours out of the five hours that the group was in session.

The other toddlers, all "normally active" in every respect, arrived at 7:30 a.m. and left after lunch. David went at 9:00 a.m. and left at 11:00, before lunch. He attended two-fifths of the time for one-half the fee.

At the end of the school year, the teachers let him stay for lunch one time. He could eat with the rest of the children…but only if I agreed to be there! The teachers must have anticipated refereeing an explosion of some sort by David. It didn't occur. David was happy to be allowed to stay. Actually, he was so awed by the occasion that his table manners were impeccable, to no one's greater surprise than mine!

Yes, teachers and children discriminated against him. This was hard for us to accept, let alone find a way to explain to David. The isolation of David from classmates was done notwithstanding all the civil rights legislation being tossed about, during the early years of the civil rights '70s.

There was a recurring experience during that year that I vividly remember. It concerned our almost daily confrontation with a two-year-old classmate of David's. To this day, it amuses and somewhat unsettles me. This particular little boy was always at the yard gate or near the front door to "greet" David and me. Dracula would have made us feel equally as welcome! And, we'd not felt half as apologetic for being there.

The little person would kick at the door when we came in sight or he'd skip the door and kick at us, announcing at the top of his young lungs, "I hate you!" "Go away!" or "Don't come back!" All the while, he'd be flailing his little fists in every direction. He seemed to be indicating the worst that would take place with Dave, as soon as the teachers and I turned our backs!

A real public relations representative for the school!

I thought it amusing to observe the way that this child was probably mimicking actions he'd undoubtedly noticed in other people or on TV. Somewhere. Perhaps he'd seen grownups doing the same thing?

At any rate, the maddening revelation for me was to learn that this child's father was a professor at OSU. Not just any old professor, either. He was the head of the speech and hearing clinic where David was receiving therapy! It would have been a great temptation, had the child been older, to tell him that if it were not for children such as David, his professor-father would not have had a job!

In spite of some less-than-pleasant moments, David loved nursery school. He seemed to try to protect himself from the verbal attacks of his peers and from the impatience of the young student-teachers. In spite of it all, he made an effort to concentrate on absorbing all he could of the arts, crafts, exercises, songs and a-b-c's during the brief class times.

For Child Development School and Exceptional Child Clinic, batteries of tests followed seemingly endless stacks of forms. I was never told if the tests were for the benefit of the child being properly evaluated, or for practice by the people who administered them. Test results were frequently so varied that they were almost never indicative of what I knew David's true abilities were.

He and I each came to dread the scrutiny such exams put us through. Those probing people who administered the tests were part of the now-nameless host who appeared, pen and stop-watch in hand, to try to categorize our son. Their own enthusiasm for the questioning was equaled only by David's dislike for each successive experience.

We'd first started with forms and testing with Dr. Simon when Dave was fifteen months old. By almost three years of age, he was growing street-wise, playing the "testing game" with the professionals. He had already discovered that some questions seemed pointless, so he would do barely enough to get the entire distasteful matter concluded…He could not have cared less about the results and what they *seemed* to reveal about him.

David and I both knew what he could and could not do, academically. However, he didn't give a whit about sharing this knowledge with inquisitive strangers who frequently hovered over him.

After being subjected to hours of questioning, he would, sooner or later, simply tune out his immediate surroundings. He would withdraw and refuse to cooperate any longer.

Test results were then evaluated by experts, i.e., people with credentials, and finally a parent conference would be scheduled. At this meeting, supposedly some light would be shed on our son's academic abilities.

Very little light was ever shed!

The conferences on academics usually ended on a note similar to those with other professionals: "Sorry, we don't know what's causing the problems. We don't have any clear-cut suggestions for you. Try somewhere else."

"Thanks a lot for your help."

"Pay the bill."

Actually, there was an agreement on one or two things:

"He obviously has some type of brain damage," which we had long since figured out for ourselves.

Or, the most hateful pronouncement of all: "You are probably the cause of his problems."

It began to sound like a broken record.

Their collective authoritative verdicts were, "He will most likely not be able to go to school. If he does, he'll never sit still in a classroom. Certainly he will never attend, much less complete, high school."

Thanks a lot!

I would be devastated, all over again.

George would be equally distressed.

David would be wondering when the next tests were going to start.

Off-hand, I can think of eight occasions when this happened, all before David was old enough for kindergarten!

Family self-esteem evaporated under the barrage of findings by the experts. We reasoned that if these professionals could offer neither an accurate diagnosis nor a recommendation for help, then what was to be done? David's chances for some sort of future in school looked increasingly more uncertain after each test.

In spite of these doomsday predictions, there were some good things happening. There was some progress in speech therapy. Sounds were becoming words. Motor skills were developing, even if it were at an almost imperceptible rate. Where once he could barely grasp large blocks, at three years of age he could hold onto all sizes and shapes of tiny Lego blocks. In return, they became his constant companions.

Even better than holding onto them, he began to be able to fasten them together, manipulating them the way he wanted, into recognizable creations.

He engineered delicately arched churches and towering office buildings, built impressive schoolhouses and busy-looking fire stations. His villages grew into cities full of fences and street lamps, shrubs and animals. No detail was overlooked as his imagination took hold. Colorful stacks of teeny blocks turned into delightful productions.

The smaller the blocks, the better the exercise for his small hands and fingers. By the time he graduated to the tiniest blocks, he was able to do amazingly detailed work such as shuttered windows that opened. He always finished off his architectural wonders with intricately landscaped grounds.

With each decrease in block size, David met a new challenge, gaining confidence in his ability to produce something esthetically pleasing. What he didn't know, was, that, he was exercising and training the many muscles that would one day enable him to write, draw, use scissors, catch a ball, and ultimately, use a computer, as well as paint and sculpt in *college* art classes.

Music, too, spoke to him as it had to me since I was a first-grader and sat in front of Mrs. Longwell's piano for my initial lesson. We bought lots of children's record albums (this was long before CDs) and spent hundreds of hours, listening and learning. It wasn't long before David could proudly read the books that accompanied the records. He would give a verbatim account of Winnie the Pooh's adventures or recall word-for-word stories as varied as *Cinderella, Frankenstein* or *Peter and the Wolf.*

He learned to tell time and tie his shoes, as well as to give his version of Biblical truths and scientific theory.

Listening, learning and growing, he tried singing and found that he could carry a tune. John would grab his drumsticks, plunk along on anything within arm's reach as he and David vocalized childish duets. What wonderful songs for my heart!

John's interest in many subjects piqued David's attention. Together, they'd thumb through George's scientific journals or through less demanding comic books. Little escaped their curiosity, so we compiled a children's library. Spanish/English readers, full of pictures, simplified to their level frequently captivated them.

Science, politics, economics…the subject didn't matter…they cared only that the quantity was endless.

Musical knowledge came from many backgrounds. The rock 'n' roll of the '60s and '70s, along with more than a little of Tom Jones, were played alongside Brahms, Bach and, my favorite, Beethoven. Our boys listened to, absorbed and enjoyed their exposure to a variety of talents.

They even discovered the sounds of normal and abnormal heartbeats, thanks to their daddy's recording from vet school, showing the difference. Using a stethoscope, listening to each other's heart sounds, was great fun for them!

The written word came alive for our sons, as they made the connection between what they heard and what they saw on a page. With this realization, David's speech therapy began to make sense to him! Mouths made sounds, sounds made words, and words were spoken and written on pages. The shapes used for writing were how the sounds looked!

After such a struggle in the beginning, David now understood that we, along with his speech and nursery school teachers, were trying to help, not torment him. His response was affirmative and immediate. He began to sense that he needed help, both for channeling his abundant energies and for assistance in academics.

CHAPTER NINE
Growth, Change, Fun

Although previously we had the assurance of the St. Louis physician who had read David's EEG, done in 1970 at Ft. Smith, Arkansas, and he was absolutely certain "that David did not actually have brain damage," common sense told us in 1971 that our child very possibly did have such damage. The doctor had misinterpreted the tests or else the results had been wrongly reported to us. Later, other professionals, whose advice and help we sought, lent credence to this same attitude.

In addition, their cumulative failure to properly diagnose his problems kept reinforcing their standardized agreement, that, somehow I caused his problems.

That was unacceptable!

We seemed to be in mortal combat with a problem that defied definition. So, we trudged on, in a life that sometimes seemed headed nowhere, only to be teased with occasional glimmers of hope.

The Mellaril medication had given David's growing young body a change of pace and a chance to slow down, so that he could more-or-less compose himself. Until he outgrew each increase in dosage.

By the time he was three years old, he needed an increase every three months. He didn't require a lot more of the drug, but the need for small increases was obvious.

In a letter to Dr. Simon, July 1971, I wrote:

David has been showing progress until the last two weeks or so. He seems now to be getting crankier, harder to handle and gets at loose ends much more quickly. Is it possible that this could be part of a pattern, that about every three months he is either building a tolerance to, or outgrowing, his dosages of Mellaril?

About this same time, John was undergoing allergy testing at Oklahoma City, adding his multiple allergies to our circumstances. Everything seemed to send him into frenzied sneezing: dust, animals, grains, etc.

I remember going home after hearing the allergist's diagnosis, instruction sheets in my hands, and sitting in John's room, crying. "Good grief, there is no way we can keep him out of touch with all of these common household items that bother him. How about the bill we owe, hundreds of dollars, just for doing the testing?" It all seemed too much for us to confront.

George and I gathered our thoughts and decided that nothing could be as awful as we imagined. We'd just try to keep him comfortable, George would give John his weekly shots and somehow we'd make it.

"Daddy, that hurts so much, but I'll stand still," four-year-old John commented as he eyed the needle and syringe heading for his small arms every Wednesday.

An extremely patient and compliant child, John even withheld complaints when George was gone and I was to give his shots…once. We were at my sister's home. Being a diabetic, she was used to giving herself shots several times daily, but balked at giving John's. Her husband had dutifully fulfilled his role as doting uncle and had given John's shot the week before. This week he was out of town and no one else was around who was willing to give John the necessary injection.

In three more days we'll be back home at Stillwater but by that time John will be overdue for his allergy shot, I guiltily thought. I put it off as long as I dared. At that time, the very sight of a needle and syringe was enough to send me into unconsciousness.

Trying to gather courage, I slowly wiped John's arm with an alcohol-soaked cotton ball. I filled the syringe with the allergy extract…and waited.

John face was turned away from me. After a moment, he slowly faced me, commenting, "Mother, if you'll just hurry up I can go back outside and play. Now, don't worry, it's not gonna hurt...you..."

Surprised at his bravery which shamed my cowardice I carefully aimed the needle into what I hoped was the right place. I injected the fluid. Fast! Before I did something perfectly dumb, such as faint!

My sister, watching from the sofa, laughed as I completed the task, paled and lay down on the floor.

Suddenly, it was no laughing matter: My sister and son were in action, coaxing me back to consciousness! Assuredly, I could not have given Florence Nightingale a run for her money!

Even little David had to chuckle at his mother's pathetic performance. Watching safely from the doorway, he drawled moral support, "It's O K, Mom."

Shortly afterward, I wrote to Dr. Simon again, following an examination of both children. He still maintained that David was a "classic hyperactive child who should show a positive response to Ritalin or Vistaril."

He had suggested that we try the Ritalin one more time, for several days. Maybe another go-round of it would prove beneficial.

I tried the Ritalin Monday and Tuesday, with every intention of using all of the five-day supply that you prescribed, but it simply did not work.

By 1:30p.m. Monday, David had been screaming for most of the day and was so unsettled that he was driving John and me up the wall! Then, from about 5:15 until 6:00 p.m., he babbled and jabbered constantly at a postcard he had gotten in the mail that day. I could not decide if it were good or bad—at least something had his attention, but he was so nervous and jumpy about it.

As the evening wore on, he began wringing his hands and showing his agitation in other ways. He was chewing on his tongue and he continued to do this all day Tuesday.

He babbled in his sleep (when he finally went to sleep) Monday night. He had been up for fourteen hours with no nap and still he fought going to sleep. He did the same thing Tuesday night.

Monday was mostly one ear-piercing screaming bout after another usually for no reason. Nothing would satisfy him, and he tore apart and hurled across the room everything that he was capable of picking up.

It reminded me of a couple of months ago when he kept running to the storm door and hitting it. Even after he was told not to, he continued, until the bottom half of the door shattered from his blows. At any rate, I decided that two days were my limit, whether or not it was his limit, so this morning (Wednesday) I put him back on the Mellaril.

He is calming down, and, compared to the past two days, is greatly improved. Of course, compared to a normal child, he is still out of control much of the time.

We don't like to depend on a drug to control his behavior, but I simply do not know what else to do to help him…

…As he grows older, it seems obvious to me that whatever brain damage he has is more in the area of behavior than in intellect. He understands almost everything that he hears…I know that he does. It's just that he does not seem to have the capacity to control his actions.

He has recognized and been able to say, on sight, the letters of the alphabet for at least three or four months, and he counts and recognizes numbers up to ten.

He will be three in September and I think that if he were retarded, he would not be responding in some of these areas. When he is in the proper mood, he follows instructions well, picks up his toys, puts them away and knows where to find his clothes in his dresser. He asks for food by its proper name at the table, and seems anxious and eager to learn.

From September 1971:

David seems to have made a great deal of progress this summer in speech. He makes many sentences…is very curious about the names of objects…will almost always try to mimic whatever is said…

His physical size makes control difficult and no one knows that better than I do…It, also, makes it difficult to reconcile his immature (and often disappointing or discouraging) actions since he physically appears to be much older than he is chronologically.

…it is a fact that he simply chooses to act in a contrary manner at times…giving the appearance of being slow.

…the previously unintelligible sounds have really begun to be formed into distinct sentences this spring, and even more this summer…he knows the names of the parts of his body…knows how to perform simple chores (which is a definite improvement over a year ago when it was a waste of time to ask him to do any simple task)…

He watches TV from his high chair, where he is gently restrained by the tray…he has started enjoying books and sits for the completion of a short story…and is possessive of his own books.

At this point his medication had reached forty-five milligrams, three times daily. This was an increase of four and a half times what he had started on, just twelve short months earlier! How much could his little body continue to tolerate without terrible results?

I noted:

David is an extraordinarily loving child and very affectionate…it's hard (for me) to love a child as he is having the zillionth violent tantrum…however, when he is punished by having to sit alone, HE snaps back quickly (more quickly than I) with hugs, kisses and a genuine desire to try harder to please.

***

To David's credit, "trying to please" is still a characteristic he possesses. Each time he "goofs," whether slightly or to the zenith, he rapidly resolves to not repeat the action. Sometimes, the resolution works, sometimes not.

When I wrote to Dr. Simon, I was teaching David the primary colors and working with both boys on learning to count 'way above ten, just doing the mothering the two pre-schoolers needed.

During relatively quiet times, George and I watched them, with intense pride in our children's accomplishments.

"What's this for, Momma?"

Distracted, I didn't answer John's question.

"Hmmm…now, if I put this into it, maybe I'll get something hooked up…"

John's one, agonized scream jolted me and I raced into the living room to find our five-year-old dazed, face down on the floor, holding his right hand next to his chest and whimpering.

The blackened electrical outlet and a darkened, still warm, soft paper clip told the story.

As I gathered him into my arms and inspected his slightly singed fingers, I asked, "What on earth did you think you were doing, John?"

"Nuthin' much…"

"Try me."

"Wel-l-l, O.K. You see, Dave and I had these little cars. We thought we could make them run faster if we hooked 'em up to the electricity...Guess I was wrong?"

"Right! You were wrong! You're just very lucky that you didn't kill yourself!"

David, observing the excitement, tried first to cheer up his injured brother, then proceeded to cheer him on!

"Hurry, do it again, John! That's FUN!"

Evidently, the streak of fire leaping from the wall socket had not only ignited the paper clip, John's hand and the paneling; it touched off David's speech center! For the first time, he put together two sentences consecutively!

Although David lagged behind his peers in speech development, he was showing some progress!

Sitting on the living room floor, my sons in my arms, I considered that his speech had been practically non-existent when he was twenty-five months old, and now, a year later, he spoke in understandable, short sentences. A miracle!

From that fiery moment, until we moved out of the mobile home six years later, that darkened wall plate remained symbolic of a big step, for both children!

Encouragement cropped up elsewhere. Both boys would watch happily when we'd add to their artistic collection covering our hall walls. Parents everywhere can identify with finger paintings and they were definitely "in" at our home for years. They provided colorful splashes in our otherwise rather dreary surroundings. The subject matter was inventive and interesting. Our feeling that both boys had artistic talent was proven correct years later.

Admittedly, a person has to be either biased or crazy to look at pre-school efforts and see a future artist. We didn't deny either characteristic. Still, the efforts were creative and sensitive to a degree that was noticeable even to visitors.

David, of course, was delighted to see that his more impulsive efforts drew the same kind of response from us as those John carried home from his nursery school and kindergarten. It was a happy time, for him to have positive acknowledgment rather than criticism.

There were other advancements. John's allergies lessened with his weekly injections. David's medication helped him maintain, although it continued to require periodic increases.

George's scholastic standings were high, and his name appeared regularly on the honor roll.

As the 1971-72 school year drew to a close, I received the dreaded phone call from the dean of the Home Ec Department. She asked me to come to her office for a conference. Even this early in our children's academic lives, I had discovered that parent-teacher conferences meant the teacher did the conferring and I did the listening!

So it was this time!

David had found participating in nursery school to be confusing, to say the least. Aside from the one child who unabashedly showed his disgust for our son, others plainly did not like him even if they more carefully disguised their dislike. Interacting on a one-to-one basis with teachers or other adults was much easier for David because he felt no competitiveness with adults.

His biggest rival was himself and he found that very difficult to tolerate: Somehow he sensed, that, no matter how hard he tried, his own performance would be second best! Consequently, he vented his frustrations in his frequently disruptive behavior.

I felt that his outbursts were his way of gaining some sort of attention, albeit negative attention. From his viewpoint, He seemed to feel that when he was naughty, people noticed him rather than other children.

It seemed that he justified his actions by believing "it doesn't matter" if the result were punishment. What did matter to him was that he was communicating his feelings to the world: He was alive, he was a person, and he wanted and needed to be noticed. Almost anything, even punishment, was better than being ignored!

Understandably, he most valued the opinions of those people who frequently ignored him: Peers, teachers and relatives. In exhaustion and desperation at home, George, John and I, also, turned away from him at times.

If a situation can't be understood, many people meet a problem head-on, by ignoring it. "Maybe it'll change…or go away…but at least I don't have to deal with it, if I don't acknowledge that it is there, in my pathway, causing me a problem!"

Also, David knew that he was not able to do many of the things that he observed other three-year-olds doing. Feeling that he was an outcast, he achieved his own kind of attention—and notoriety—by exhibiting often-outrageous behavior.

This was the situation that had prompted the phone call from the dean. In her office, she informed me, as gently I'm sure as she was able to, that David would not be accepted for a second year at the OSU nursery school. Now, that was rather a slap in the face to me as a parent. Usually, once a child attended the OSU nursery school, it was a fact that the child would continue until he was ready for kindergarten.

This latest revelation wasn't a surprise, however. In fact, I was amazed that they had allowed him to complete two semesters! I had seen the faces of the student-teachers, looking much the same as the small students did, showing dislike for David.

Mercifully, David appeared oblivious to their behavior quirks. Of course he wasn't, but he handled their bad manners with more compassion than they handled his!

Naturally, he had feelings about the way the nursery school students and teachers reacted to him. Easily and all-too-frequently, unkind reactions toward him reinforced each other.

Responding to the negative attitudes of adults and other children, David began a process of insulating himself from his surroundings when circumstances became too much for him to handle…when he could not meet the demands made of him…freeing himself from discouraging actions directed toward him. His device was self-preservation by feigned indifference. It may be one reason why he is still sane. His own protective barrier helped to stabilize his shaky self-esteem when it dropped to low points.

He now says that from his perspective as an adult, it helps to share with other people his emotions about himself, "God made me the way I am and he made other people the way they are…and none of us needs to prove anything to anyone else!"

What a precious lesson he learned, and now teaches!

CHAPTER TEN
A Christmas to Remember

When David was three years old, even though his intellectual progress showed amazing strides, his social development was less than desirable.

I knew, without a doubt: This child is not retarded. I recognized Dave's bright responses and a great desire to learn. George agreed. Damage was apparent in three areas, but otherwise he was a child who could be taught and who could learn.

The problem was that traditional teaching methods just did not work. The efforts that George and I were making by talking with teachers, administrators and other experts about how to best help David were not always met with open minds. Very often there were no charitable attitudes, but we never allowed those responses to force us to quit trying!

High fevers plagued Dave when he was an infant and toddler. They attacked without warning or reason. Suddenly, dramatically, his temperature would soar from normal to 104 in fifteen minutes, remain there for approximately forty-eight hours and, just as dramatically, subside. The usual measures didn't help to bring down the fever. We just had to wait until it went down. Doctors showed no unusual concern when we told them about the fever-events.

Somehow, it didn't seem fair that one small body should be forced to cope with so many circumstances beyond control or comprehension.

Before David was born, my husband and I shared the usual fairy-tale visions of watching two "normal" children of "normal" abilities grow into "normal" adults. We thought of "normal" as a person not causing any waves and not having too many problems, able to live independently and productively. We imagined that a "normal" person would fit the dictionary definition of "usual or ordinary, characterized by average growth or intelligence, healthy in mind and body." No deviations up or down from the standard.

Decades later, we believe that we would not have traded either of our wonderfully exceptional sons for a half dozen normal, average, typical, ordinary children! We know that ours are above the crowd and stand out...and we're definitely proud of them!

Reaching this acceptance was a rocky road. We had little time for ourselves with no day or week passing without the responsibilities of rearing one child who was brain damaged and another who was gifted.

In fact, it seemed that not even twenty-four hours would pass without someone complaining about David...Sunday school teachers, schoolteachers, and parents of other children, friends and relatives. Most of the fussing was done under the guise of, "I'm telling you this in order to help you and David..." followed by a detailed account of his most recent infractions.

We felt our lives were a series of stomping-out-one-fire-while-two-more-were-ignited with David forever at the center of the inferno. There were occasional times, of course, when things cooled off somewhat. Humorous situations occurred, even if they were not funny at the time. They do make us smile after the fact. Perspective is a great balm for emotional wounds. Feelings heal and sensitive natures retreat.

Christmas, 1972, provided us with one of those tell-it-over-and-over stories. George was in his final year in veterinary school...thank goodness! We hoped—and believed—this would be our final holiday in the steadily shrinking trailer house.

He and the boys had "liberated" a lonesome cedar tree from an otherwise empty field outside of town near our home. We felt certain that the person from whose land it was taken wouldn't mind his unknown donation to our holiday, for we could not afford to buy a tree and no one lived near the land. The field-mates for this tree had already been sprayed and destroyed by the owner and this survivor wouldn't last when plowing started in the spring. We rationalized that we had helped the owner of this property be rid of this stubborn holdout.

The tree was a work of nature's art. Beautifully shaped and bright-green lovely, upright in one corner of our tiny living room, it proudly displayed its sparkling lights and colorful decorations.

It was a bit awesome, larger than we could have anticipated when it was still in the field. Ceiling-high, it also bulged forth onto surrounding furniture, but that didn't matter. Maybe an abundance of tree would help us forget the small number of presents!

The children were delighted. Surely, Santa couldn't possibly bypass so gorgeous a creation!

The household assumed a festive, expectant air, and I made cookies and candies from a dwindling supply of staples.

Between cooking projects, I often worked until the wee hours of the morning, typing for students.

Late at night, sitting alone at the typewriter, I appreciated the warmth and loveliness of the nearby glowing tree. It seemed to be an encouraging friend, growing more familiar as the holidays approached.

The provocative appeal of the holiday tree may have been its own undoing!

With Christmas barely days away, David and disaster struck! Talking on the phone to a typing client, I turned my back to the tree. At the same time, temptation overwhelmed the four-year-old. He'd daily been admiring the tree from his diminutive point of view, always cautioned to not reach too high to rearrange the ornaments. Throwing caution to the wind, David decided to have a closer look.

Much closer.

On his own level.

He grabbed a protruding branch, gave a hearty tug—and the unbalanced tree crashed to the carpet!

Startled by the sound of breaking glass, I hung up the phone, turned...and saw David wearing his usual amazed expression as he viewed the scene: cedar needles, shattered ornaments and lights...everywhere. The living room was filled diagonally with a spectacular amount of greenery and glass.

For me, this was the last straw!

I grabbed the phone again, dialed my dear, sympathetic friend, Jaryl Everist, and hardly let her say hello. I gave her a brief account of this latest escapade.

"Carolyn, why don't you come on over and we'll talk about it?"

"Talk! Talk? Good grief, Jaryl, there's no time to talk! I've got thirty more pages to type on this guy's doctoral dissertation and it's due tomorrow and there's the biggest mess I've ever seen all over the living room…"

"Come over, anyway. You sound like the whole world just crashed on your floor and I can hear David, crying. Surely, it's not the end of everything…although, you *do* sound like it is…"

I kept interrupting her to pour out my sad tale, and she kept interrupting, trying to calm me.

The best solution seemed to be to clear up the mess, and then at least I wouldn't have to look at it.

"Alright, that's a start."

I hurriedly ask if she'd "mind taking care of David for a while"…maybe give him some refuge from my current feelings…then I headed out the door with him.

Jaryl had no time to answer. I arrived at her driveway in two minutes!

Out of patience, I slid the car to a stop, threw it into "park" and shoved David out the door into Jaryl's waiting arms, then pushed it into gear and sailed back home. The entire trip couldn't have taken more than five minutes, but it should have, considering the distance between our houses!

With David at a safe distance, I faced the wreckage: Resurrection seemed improbable as I surveyed the remains of the tree and ornaments. The demise appeared to be permanent. I reluctantly transferred the shambles out the front door, down the steps and to the front gate.

George could haul it away. Later.

That there could be a backlash from my actions never occurred to me. The Christmas mood had just abruptly ended for me. As far as I was concerned, the holidays were history, and it was only December 22nd!

Suppertime…and my husband arrived simultaneously.

All afternoon I'd heard, "Momma, what's the tree doing in the yard?" "Can't we just fix it up?"

"Why's the carpet all wet and full of glass?" John had returned from school, shocked at the sight of Christmas Past.

"How?" "Why?" "Can't we" …Good grief! I had to start explanations all over, again, for George.

He surveyed the scene, indoors and out.

"Well, I think the tree still basically looks O.K. Just minus a branch or two and some needles."

"No, it doesn't look O.K. Besides, you didn't have to clean up the mess!"

"Oh, come on, now. No one tosses out a tree before Christmas!"

"This someone does!"

"You're just being stubborn! Let's get the tree back in the house…" George's pleading, accented by John's begging, was reaching a crescendo.

"I'll not have that tree back in here! David will probably just yank it down, again. Once is enough! More than enough!" My volume matched his.

I stormed into the kitchen to finish fixing supper.

In a conspiracy, George and the boys grabbed coats, hats, and gloves and headed for the lonesome tree, sadly fluttering tinseled branches in the December air. It was cold and dark outside.

Fifteen minutes passed and the trio returned, proudly displaying the results of their restoration efforts: the top half of the tree!

"Now then, we can set this on the corner table, decorate it and we'll be back in business tonight," George declared as he and John refilled the tree stand with water.

I didn't want to further alienate my young family and, certainly, this close to Christmas I should try to stay in their good graces. I acquiesced. An olive branch was extended that night in the form of redecorating the tree, replacing the few gifts around it and allowing the boys each an extra Christmas cookie.

Averting panic in our home often required three character facets: the patience of a saint, the wisdom of a diplomat and the temperament of a dictator. The first two qualities I possessed in only the most modest quantity. The third was ever-present.

Somehow, on that wintry evening, those three traits sorted themselves into better proportions and we survived. As bedtime approached, we were trading stories of other "Adventures of David."

I recalled a lazy springtime afternoon a couple of years earlier when I was taking advantage of the peacefulness of John and David's naptime. Outdoors, I perched on the porch step, watching the birds building new homesteads.

My reverie was cut short by an unfamiliar scraping sound behind me. Surprised, I turned…and caught sight of the back bedroom window screen flying away from the trailer! Immediately, chubby arms and legs came propelling through the open space where the screen had been. Freedom from naptime was only seconds away for David!

He didn't see me, as he rappelled down the side of the trailer. He was hanging onto the crib sheet he'd hastily dismantled from his bed and which was mercifully caught under a corner of the mattress. He looked just the way I'd imagined an Alpine climber would, and seemed just as experienced!

Suddenly, he let go, too far from the ground, and landed in a dusty, breathless, unhurt heap on the grass. That child was all grins and giggles. I, on the other hand, was ready for a straightjacket as I hunted up a ladder and replaced the now-bulging and stretched screen. David had suffered no problem any more serious than dust on his diaper!

Of course, David wasn't always the culprit in heart-stopping shenanigans: John had given George and me plenty of pauses, also. So did several babysitters.

There was the time that George and I returned to find the boys asleep, as they should have been, and the sitter calmly watching TV…and the lower window on the storm door, shattered, with the remnants in a scattered trail down the porch steps. Obviously, the cause of the damage was the glass-encrusted orange, lying in its own juice, on the front porch. It seemed, when we finally got all three versions of the story fitted together, that the boys had been playing catch using—what else?—the orange instead of a ball. They were indoors, but before long the orange was outdoors, alone. Orange, one; door, zero.

And, there was the night that the boys and a now nameless sitter enjoyed a refreshing evening of games and popcorn. Certainly, it sounded harmless enough in the planning stage. We had no idea that the sitter's kitchen skills were low priority when we gave permission for her to fix refreshments.

I assumed that anyone old enough to fix popcorn would be able to follow the instructions that were plainly printed on the side of the electric popper. It was uncomplicated each time we used it: Pour in a measured amount of popcorn to the "fill" line, add the plastic cover, plug it in, and wait…

Not so!

Somehow, the sitter translated "fill" to "full" and that appeared to be exactly what she had done: filled the container FULL of explosive kernels, plugged it in…and probably ran for cover!

Popcorn adhered to the kitchen ceiling in cloud-like bundles…stuck to the paneled walls…covered the carpeted floor like so much snow refusing to melt. The stuff layered the forty-eight-inch diameter dining table, flowing conspicuously over the edge, providing both texture and sound as we crunched it with bare feet. It may have been the only full bag of popcorn kernels in history in which every single kernel popped!

The sitter evaporated before we discovered the full impact of her evening with the boys. Our Precious Angels remained suspiciously "sound asleep" during the cleanup.

Instances such as these helped put life in perspective, in spite of the few problems they caused, as we felt that somehow we were less unique and more like everyone else with our family.

Once in a while, we would be lulled in a sort of complacency, while the storminess of our life stilled briefly. George and I would feel that, maybe, we four were not so different, after all.

Usually, the calm simply preceded another upheaval. At least, for a few hours or days, we had some space in which to re-group for the impending tidal wave that was sure to come flooding in.

In those quieter moments, we afforded ourselves the luxury of "Let's Pretend," dreaming that our lives would somehow settle into the dull, daily routine that many families have. We would have welcomed dull!

Pretending was entertaining. Reality, however, was something very different!

CHAPTER ELEVEN
Graduating to Real Life

It was spring 1973. George's graduation was approaching and it seemed that the almost impossible goal from 1968, surviving veterinary school, was in sight.

The popular pastime of '70s college students—sit-ins and campus rioting—was subsiding. Coeds still paraded around in attention-getting very-mini-skirts and see-through blouses. Overalls, minus shirts—the uniform of the day—provided "scenic" decorations on campus, when worn by either gender.

The "cowboys" congregating in front of Ag Hall continued their time-honored diversion of jousting for position at the foot of the stairway, watching the form-fitting jeans that stretched over the procession of "cowgirls" ascending to classes.

Normal campus.

Oklahoma State is famous for its gorgeous landscaping, which was bursting into copious and colorful displays, each outdoing the neighboring ones. They were a delight to the eyes and the spirit, alerting everyone that spring was alive and well.

It was the time of rebirth, new challenge and renewal, with days full of planning and hope.

Our family's eyes were on the future, also: At last, George would be able to pursue his new profession. We would be able to have a real house, rather than one sitting on wheels.

John, completing first grade at St. Francis School, seemed ready to take on the world.

David, less eager but still excited, also sensed those changes were approaching and he was anxious to be a special part of them. He was completing his third year of speech therapy, while John was finishing up a year in speech therapy, also.

Our older son had acquired a lisp and we knew that therapy would help him to be rid of it before it became an embarrassment for him. It was kind of cute on a six-year-old…but we knew he would not think it cute when he became a grown man!

Each child was doing particularly well in his own school. John had several young friends and David had even managed to gain the friendship of one classmate.

Things seemed on more of an even keel than they had ever been for us. So, we were not in the least prepared for what happened.

For a year, George and I had discussed our hope that, before leaving Stillwater, testing of some kind would be done for David and that the testing would give us a clue about what to do next to help him. Although we had single-handedly sought testing and no help resulted, we were undaunted as we continued to seek professional expertise. With the exception of Dr. Simon, most other expert advice had been non-existent.

David and I had completed six months of once-a-week sessions at the local mental health center, attempting to discover the root of his behavior problems. The personnel of the OSU speech and hearing clinic had persuaded me to do this. No one seemed in agreement with my husband and myself that David's problems resulted from a physical core of brain damage and that his emotional exceptionalities were the effect, not the cause, of what was happening to him. Answers from professionals took on an almost unbearable sameness: His difficulties stemmed from emotional trauma…caused by me!

The mental health counselors, after video taping David and me in numerous situations for several months, then discussing and counseling, suggested that we go to the University of Oklahoma Child Study Center in Oklahoma City. The Center was part of the OU Medical School and it was hoped that something could be discovered that might be helpful. It seemed to be a logical step.

Following the initial contact and the predictable forms at the center, we were told that it would be at least five months before David could be seen there. The results and heartache of the three subsequent, futile trips were related in the prologue of this book.

Yes, we were discouraged, but not defeated. We simply renewed our effort after we found no help at the center.

No one else would encourage us, so we tried to boost our own spirits. We bolstered ourselves when no one else would. We told ourselves that David would grow up going to school like other children. He would become a useful person, happy about himself and his work.

We realized, more than ever, that he was an intelligent person, capable of learning. He was not a withering vegetable to be cast aside and forgotten, in spite of what the "experts" said!

We practically spoon-fed ourselves on these positive attitudes the winter of 1973. David had already proven that he could and would learn, even under the most difficult circumstances of his hyperactivity, the Mellaril and teachers who did not really understand how to teach him!

The wonder of it was that the drug didn't dull his brain to the point that he could not learn!

No amount of negative attitude from medical persons or educators lessened our determination to see that David was educated. We had two bright sons and we were going to do all that we could to see that each child was taught as competently as possible and for as long as he desired to attend school.

What a rough road remained!

Naturally, we were only human and there were times when we wondered if we were deluding ourselves and expecting too much…desiring the unattainable…but even at those times, we knew that we could never give up!

Both children had inquisitive minds, which kept George and me on our toes. While John's motor skills were developing at a gallop and he could do all of the right things in the proper sequence, as one birthday passed another, David's motor skills were a hindrance.

He was four years old and still had difficulty catching or throwing a ball, walking a balance beam or going up and down stairs with alternating feet. His stair climbing and descending was done slowly, two feet per step. His major accomplishment had been with the tiny building blocks.

The hyperactivity remained more or less controlled but required those ever-increasing Mellaril doses to help him not be in motion every second.

More obvious improvement was in his speech development, as he was able to carry on typical childish conversations. Many sounds were difficult or impossible for him, but at least he could make a great many of his desires known. And, we knew that with enough correctional work over a long enough period, with patience on the part of David as well as his instructors, he would eventually be able to speak without difficulty.

We began to notice, in his speech patterns, that when he could not retrieve a word from his memory, and could not say exactly what he wanted, that he was always able to give accurate enough definitions that his listener could supply the missing word. It was a rewarding discovery to find that his vocabulary was as varied and precise as that of a child who was several years older and more sophisticated.

He paid remarkably close attention to all discussions in the household, whether he understood the topic or not, and he seemed to retain much of what he observed.

Books still claimed his fascinated attention, if only for brief interludes. He and John developed brotherly attitudes in playing out their make-believe stories, so we shared the trailer and yard with all sorts of cowboys, Indians, spacemen and a variety of creepy, crawly, fanciful and live creatures. There were no dull moments!

John, who also enjoyed building all sorts of new creations, gathered pieces of abandoned boards, some of Daddy's nails and "liberated" a hammer from my kitchen, intending to make a playhouse for himself and his brother. By the time the building was completed, George had joined the effort and the entire construction was substantial enough for the two children and our cat to not only sit in but on!

Painted bright red and sporting an attic, it provided hours of entertainment opportunities for the boys, and was a forerunner of a magnificent, genuine log cabin which George built for them a few years later.

By paying attention to what David was and was not learning, and by reading books and articles, we learned about damage to the area of the brain that affords a person the ability to understand abstract concepts. Mathematics is such a concept and was difficult for David.

David's low math skills plagued him continually, once he started to school, and to this day can be a discouragement for him. When he was just in elementary school, however, his low performance in this area, as in the other areas affected by the brain damage, were often mis-understood by persons who had not the foggiest notion why he could do well in one subject and underachieve in another.

Given the premise that most people can understand basic math in their primary years, it was extremely difficult for many people, teachers included, to comprehend David's dilemma.

More often than not, his failure to learn was attributed by the instructors to bad attitude or bad behavior or "he just doesn't want to learn." The teachers were seldom able to grasp any knowledge of the intricate inner workings of the brain, which no doubt is tough to understand for even the best-educated medical experts.

We found that in David's case, and in the case of many other brain-damaged persons, the undamaged portions of the brain must be trained to take over the function for the damaged part. That's a real mountain to climb and requires years of grueling work to accomplish.

"Lord, if all of those 'smart' people can't help our son very much, and if George and I are only able to guess at what should be done for him, what's going to happen to him? It's up to You...

"Help us!

"Help us to help him!"

It became a litany, repeated consistently each day. Repeated until it fused into every moment of the day.

"Help us to help both of our sons. Their lives can mean so much to many people. Surely, You didn't put them on earth to just slip through life, unnoticed. They count for something!"

And, with the years, assurance and confirmation have come to us that we were right! It had to be, however, in the Lord's own way, in His own time. His timing is not our timing. We have to be patient.

Today, we are confident that we made the correct decision to not place David in an institution. There were times when we were the only people who agreed with that determination.

We are certain that we took the only path we could have taken...to help him. We armed ourselves with nothing more than love for our children, then proceeded to do combat with physicians, teachers, principals, psychiatrists, and Sunday school teachers, to name a few.

Many changes occurred in the attitude of other people, as well as changes in us. Where we once naively thought that someday David's struggle would end and we would all "live happily ever after" we found that we could live happily, even with problems!

Confrontations and anxieties often make up much of the thread from which lives are woven. What happens with, and because of, them makes life either a beautifully constructed, whole pattern or a misdirected, meaningless hodge-podge of mistakes. We aimed for the sensitive, rewarding, whole pattern.

One of the aspects of daily living that gave us many anxious moments was with the Mellaril medication. We realized as we read the insert in the medicine bottle that the drug had the possibility to do more damage than good to his body.

I shared our concerns with Dr. Simon during the summer of 1973:

David is almost five years old and is now getting 330 to 350 milligrams of Mellaril daily. Some days are quite good, and others…!

By this time, he was on a massive dosage regimen. The warnings accompanying the medication were specific and frightening. We hoped and prayed that they were not prophetic. Had the medication ever caused a bad reaction, it would have been without warning, drastic, and, perhaps, irreversible. We realized that he could be even further brain damaged. Knowing this sent chills through me every time I gave him a dose. In fact, each of his 1,095 doses per year was trauma-time for George and me.

"Is it, really, worth risking him? While we are trying to help him, could we be sentencing him to a lifetime of seizures? How would we feel, knowing what we have learned about the possibilities, if he became a palsied cripple? What would happen to him, and to us?"

Even knowing that we were medicating him because we loved and wanted to help him was of little comfort.

The questions taunted us…three times every day.

Regardless, there still seemed little else we could do. Mellaril was it. Without it, the battle, and the war, would have been lost.

Other side effects were obvious: David gained weight at an above-normal rate. He learned, slowly and often painfully, that he couldn't devour the contents of the refrigerator, pantry and kitchen cabinet in a single afternoon! His consuming thirst was awesome and he devised ingenious methods to circumvent our best efforts to keep him away from too much food and liquid.

Sooner or later—and usually sooner—he'd be caught, committing gastronomic transgressions to a phenomenal degree. For years, we carried on a spirited battle of wits with David winning far more often than we did!

Three months before his fifth birthday, we entered a different phase of family life, moving from Stillwater and the sheltered, if impoverished, school environment. Our new hometown was Weatherford, Oklahoma, where George was ready to establish his professional practice.

New life, new challenges.

David had recovered from a broken arm that had occurred when he and John were both on a horse and David, not caring for the ride, dismounted suddenly, taking his unsuspecting brother with him. John landed on David's arm, breaking both the radius and the ulna.

A chickenpox bout for both of them had come and gone, more or less uneventfully; and mumps (although they'd been vaccinated for that disease) which they shared with us was next.

Practically nothing slowed down the boys, no matter how exhausted George and I were. We were hardly relocated, still in our trailer house near town, when we started construction on our veterinary hospital. We'd made a down payment on eighty acres that would prove to be a great investment.

Summer's greenness became the gold and yellow of fall, and soon winter winds brought a snowy blanket to cover our world, halting the construction work. By mid-winter, the weather was milder and George's brother, John Paul, J.P., an expert code welder, was busily working on cattle chutes and pens in the back of the clinic building. For three months he labored alongside George, completing the home for our first professional practice.

The little boys grew used to spending spare time as impartial sidewalk superintendents, carrying nails and imitating the actions of the grownups who were too busy to pay attention to their antics.

When we did find time to see that the children were still in the county, we'd find them trying to make their own buildings and sidewalks, covered head to toe with grime, and loving it.

Spring arrived and the building was finished. We hauled used human equipment, purchased at hospital auctions, into the clinic. At the same time, salesmen for drug companies discovered us, as we went further into debt, and tried to make a living. It was a three-ring circus, most of the time, and not as economically thriving as we'd hoped, but we diligently stayed with the practice.

Imagine if you will, the first months, scurrying around to furnish the clinic. Our interim clinic was located inside the old hanger building on the property. While we waited for the new construction to be concluded, we had clients and patients seeking our help in temporary surroundings which were sparse indeed. We partially covered the original dirt floor with concrete, giving us a small, cleaner area in which to do exams and surgeries. Long corrugated sheets of metal helped keep rain off the pet cages, supplies and instruments.

Lacking post-surgical facilities, we often took dogs and cats directly from surgery at the clinic to the living room of our trailer house. If needed, we let them sleep at the foot of our bed as they awakened from anesthesia. More than once, very late at night, we even did surgery on our little living room floor, poised on our knees above the anesthetized animals.

In these primitive surroundings, it wasn't long before clients began calling my husband "Abe," as his dark beard, lanky appearance and dirt floor reminded them of a more famous American who also tried to rise above his original circumstances.

Long hours at the hospital meant short hours at home, so the boys were always underfoot at work. They, and I, learned how to clean animal cages and to assist in surgery. They practiced answering the phone very professionally. It was a true family practice.

Two weeks short of his fifth birthday, we enrolled David in kindergarten. John was starting second grade and David kept saying that he wanted to go to school, too.

There were his problems, which we discussed with the superintendent before enrollment. We were encouraged to go ahead…the kindergarten teacher was a patient young woman who would make every effort to get him off to a good start. And, the administrator had advanced degrees in special education, so surely he should know.

Frankly, we were surprised at this man's willingness to place David in a classroom. Then, we remembered that he would not be the teacher! The day-to-day bedlam would be in someone else's domain.

After hearing about some of David's more difficult areas, including his inability to correctly hold a pencil, draw a circle or make to intersecting lines on a piece of paper, the kindly administrator still insisted that we give our child the benefit of trying.

David was at the age when normal children not only do these things, but have already been doing them for a considerable time. However, the superintendent and the teacher were at least willing to work, so, on a sunny August morning, David started a new phase of his life.

CHAPTER TWELVE
Education with a Price

What a day it was! David's first experience at East Elementary, Weatherford, Oklahoma. I will always wonder what the beautiful, blonde, newly graduated teacher was thinking when we entered her classroom. I doubt that even with all of her college training she was prepared for such a sight as greeted her that morning.

There they were: A roomful of shiny, eager young faces, freshly scrubbed, emerging from babyhood...everyone dressed in brand new school togs...awaiting the knowledge that the pretty teacher would share with them during the year.

All of a sudden, there was one screaming, resistant youngster coming through the doorway, being hauled along by his mother! I was, literally, pulling and dragging my sturdy son. Attempting to enter the classroom, we faced the amazed expressions of the other students. The children pondered each step of our way and watched as David firmly planted his feet—first on the outside steps and then on the threshold, stuck in each position as if he were glued into place.

David didn't "stall" quietly, either!

Accompanying each movement that forced him further into the classroom was his protesting roar announcing very clearly that he did not want to go into the room. His idea seemed to be to prolong this adventure as actively, vocally and as long as he possibly could.

A couple of very extended minutes ticked past.

At last, we were finally inside the cheerfully decorated room. Exhausted, I could no longer hang onto his gyrating body. David lunged from my grasp and slung himself onto the floor with a ferocity that shocked me.

He pounded the floor with his fists, kicked in every direction—and that was especially tough on my shins since his new school shoes sported hard, unyielding soles!

All the while, he tearlessly snarled and wailed his woes to the startled, but silent, classmates. As David paused to catch his breath, the teacher approached him. He barely glanced at her and resumed his complaints.

Embarrassed and discouraged by his performance, I explained to Mrs. Bruton, "This is David...you've heard about him...he will be in your classroom. I'm so sorry to disrupt everything, but I didn't know this would happen. Maybe, if you talk to him, he'll believe that you and the children want him in here...and that the children will be glad to have him for a classmate. He's had some bad school experiences, already. Maybe that's what's wrong."

I hastily concluded, "If he's too much of a challenge today, I'll just take him back home. Maybe it's too early to try a 'regular' classroom. Should we wait another year?"

Introductions out of the way and apologies acknowledged, Mrs. Bruton boldly accepted the challenge of David. As I look back on that scenario, I recall my genuine admiration for the courage with which she stated, "Of course he can stay. He should stay...and we will get along!"

I thought to myself, *Her assurances must come from confidence born of inexperience!*

"David! David! Listen!" She tried to get his attention.

"See the other boys and girls. They're your friends. They really want you in this room. But, you will have to be quieter than you are now," she calmly stated as she offered her friendship. "We're going to have such a good time. See, how we've fixed up the walls with the pictures. You'll like being in here with us."

More wild movements from David.

"Please, stop kicking...We really do want you in here with us."

As suddenly as it had begun, the storm subsided. David dissolved into a sobbing heap on the floor, exhausted by his maneuvering. Curious about the kind, soft voice, with its whispered promises of peer acceptance and fun, he became attentive.

At last, he relaxed and looked around. Inquiring young faces circled him from every vantage point. Kindergartners elbowed each other to get closer. Children tried to gain a front row perspective on this stranger who was supposed to be one of them for the next nine months.

David began to notice his surroundings for the first time, giving a quiet nod of approval as he smiled and reached for Mrs. Bruton. She gathered him close to her and they made their first mutual appraisals. Each seemed to agree that the other was O.K.

Thank you, Lord, at least he's taken another step in the right direction, I prayed silently as I left the room while my son's attention was elsewhere.

Although head-to-head encounters were frequent between pupil and instructor, David and Mrs. Bruton alternately taught and learned from each other during the ensuing school year.

Each combatant frequently, stubbornly, refused to yield his or her position. Unwilling to abandon his attention-getting behavior patterns, David became a frequent guest in the principal's office. Because the principal, Mr. Johnson, had grown up only one block away from my childhood home, he seemed to feel a very special empathy with David and me.

My role as a non-classroom participant continued, as questions of David's discipline and classroom decorum arose almost daily. Often, a phone call from the teacher or the principal resolved the problems. Other, more abrasive confrontations required that I trek to the school and accompany David home.

It wasn't as though I had any answers to the riddles, but when the teacher and principal ran out of other "solutions," I was it!

Sending David home was a last resort, but it became more frequent as the year progressed.

George and I were in the midst of the crisis of trying to establish a veterinary practice from scratch, in an area where we were both unknown. Days would pass. We would have only one person, maybe two, call for assistance. No calls meant no income and our overhead continued.

My husband and I were continuing the pattern that we had established several years earlier: We worked together, helping each other, in whatever situations we found ourselves. As we had almost no income, we had no employees. We did everything ourselves, from cleaning kennels to janitorial work to autoclaving instruments to bookkeeping, such as it was.

I did the receptionist/bookkeeping/assistant tasks while George doctored the patients. The sight of bleeding limbs and bodies, which previously had me keel over on the floor, became commonplace. I rapidly learned to assist him in surgery while remaining upright and conscious!

From early morning until long after dark, we worked at the clinic, as the practice began to grow. The boys got off the bus in the afternoon and immediately turned into kennel personnel. John, just tall enough to see over the surgery table while standing on a booster chair, absorbed interesting new knowledge each time that he assisted his dad.

From the time he was three years old, he had gone to anatomy lab with George who spent evenings studying and dissecting cadavers at school. John mimicked the Latin and Greek medical language that George spoke. It wasn't long before he impressed George's veterinary classmates with his knowledge of canine and feline muscle and skeletal systems.

By the time he passed his seventh birthday, John was becoming an effective member of our medical staff.

David tried his hand, too, working in the clinic. More often than not, he had difficulty in the kennels when animals challenged him and he either became frightened or aggravated. The passage of time soothed his fears and irritation, and today, he's a tender, compassionate caretaker for the pets who've made themselves at home at his home.

Starting our practice in 1973, with David in kindergarten and John in second grade, things were far from being a bed of roses.

We were buying eighty acres of farmland just outside of Weatherford. Still living in our mobile home, constructing the clinic as well as trying to repay student loans...all left very little with which to buy necessities.

Our finances fell to an unimaginable low. Deficit spending seemed to be not only a problem with the U.S. government, but with us, also. George and I felt that if this first year in practice were not a success, little else would prosper for us.

The ritual phone calls from David's school didn't help. We were concerned that David's entire academic future could be in jeopardy. Hopefully, he would settle into the kindergarten atmosphere and be able to participate in subsequent classrooms. We had been given plenty of prophecies to the contrary, but we chose to believe our hearts rather than the other people who regularly predicted failure.

Defeat in kindergarten would have frustrated future efforts to have him accepted as a student in public schools. We were acutely aware of that. We were also certain that we had to do everything possible to help the year go as smoothly as possible both for him and for his teacher.

Had that crucial year collapsed, there would have been little that our son could have expected academically, except to look forward to a lifetime of tutors, provided that capable, willing ones could even be found.

Worse, the alternative might be narrowed and he would have to be institutionalized! That thought galvanized us! We forced ourselves to believe that the year would be successful!

Public school was a must for him, because private educational facilities were out of the question. Very few were available in Oklahoma and the ones that existed were boarding schools, very expensive and far from our home.

Thankfully, in spite of some upsets, most of the year was a good experience for all of us…discounting David's record-setting number of visits to the principal's office.

He developed a love and admiration for teachers that endures today. The thanks for that goes to Mrs. Bruton. She was as kind as she was lovely, an inspiration for David and us. We remembered her courage, each subsequent August at enrollment time!

Regretfully, that good beginning didn't continue. After the usual testing was completed the following autumn, David was placed in a self-contained special education program for first graders. We quickly discovered that "self-contained" translated to "segregated." The special education children spent their entire school day separated from the "normal" children. That situation lent itself to ongoing ridicule from peers, on the playground and in the classroom. Humiliation became a way of life for David and his special classmates.

The "normal" children might not have intended to be as cruel as they were, but the results were what counted.

David and the other special youngsters found themselves to be the victims of diminishing self-worth. They were the objects of name-calling and harsh jokes. It's probably not unusual where outspoken children are involved, but it was unusual in directness and ferocity. Equally harsh were the effects of "normal" students conspicuously ignoring them in the halls and on the playground. Either way, taunted or ignored, hurt feelings were a daily occurrence. Non-handicapped children kept themselves apart from special ed classes. Therefore, they were unaware of the unasked-for problems as well as the achievements of the special kids. The collective coolness toward special students apparently resulted from three kinds of ignorance: that of the students, their teachers and their parents. Each group appeared to feel that they should treat the special kids so horribly that they'd be either thankful to be away from the normal children, or else ridicule them because of their problems if they had to be in school.

It didn't appear to cross their collective minds to offer help or friendship…even to talk to the special students. Ignore or treat hatefully. That was that!

We shared David's daily bewilderment and distress as he returned from school, full of tales of the day's activities. It hurt us to hear about the treatment by the other children but we knew nothing to do to change their actions. We let him say what he felt, hoping that if he were allowed to vent his frustrations, he would have less permanent psychological damage than if he pushed the feelings deep inside.

Recounting his experiences, David's pain would be very real on his face and in his voice, as he discussed how the "undamaged" (his method of identification) kids acted as if the special kids could not hear, feel or absorb their viciousness.

Anyone continually subjected to such aggression will probably, predictably react defensively. That's exactly what David did!

His defensive action frequently assumed proportions of outright hostility. Gradually, given the slightest chance, David would bang an offender over the head, shove him to the ground, or box him with his fists, perhaps over-reacting to an offense. He did it in spite of our having told him and John not to fight…especially at school. Occasionally, he'd resort to making his point by using whatever weapon was handy: A book, pencil, chairs, toy…anything within arm's reach.

More than one loudmouth closed the school day with a David-inflicted "knowledge knot."

Usually, the victim was an older elementary student, for the first and second graders hadn't perfected their skills in cruelty to the obnoxious point of the third through sixth graders.

David's brand of justice was impartially meted out. Friends and foes eventually were "corrected." He emerged from first grade with a reputation as "the kid to avoid."

His actions set off phone calls from the schoolhouse! Our son began to rack up another impressive tally of trips to the office of the new principal, Tom Gage. Red-haired, always smiling, exuding the energy of his own youth along with his love for children, Tom was patience in a three-piece suit.

For all of his agreeableness, I didn't like hearing his voice when I answered the phone at the clinic.

"Mrs. Kendall, I need to talk to you...again."

My apprehension always increased in direct proportion to the amount of concern or excitement I detected in his voice.

We talked.

Often.

And at length.

And, often with a silver lining peeking through the clouds.

Even when the principal was discharging his distasteful duty of telling us about our erring offspring, Tom was a delight! He struggled to appear very strict and in control, but his love and concern for David unfailingly surfaced. Tom was one of the few people who cared enough to dig deeply and discover the lonely, frightened child who could so easily become lost to family, friends, society.

Tom's wisdom overcame his lack of experience in working with special children and eased us over many rough places that year. He labored in David's behalf far above and beyond the efforts called for by his position as principal. He counseled, listened, sympathized, and, when all else failed, punished. With care, trying to preserve the infinitely meager dignity that David was trying to nourish.

Mutual respect budded and blossomed between the long-suffering principal and our controversial child.

David's continual attention-seeking behavior assured him of repeated meetings in Tom's office. And, they were not always such bad get-togethers!

For instance, there was the day that David's teacher, in tears, called me. Surprised to hear from her rather than from Tom, I stopped supper preparations and listened intently. I assumed that our first-grader had committed some infraction worthy of my undivided attention, judging by the subdued quality of his teacher's voice, plus the fact that she was crying.

Yes, he'd been sent to Mr. Gage's office that afternoon. The school year was near its end so the routine was familiar to David and Tom. The principal, disliking the corporal punishment that was legal to administer to his elementary students, often chose to discuss the problems and avoid having to physically correct the child.

During the talks, David had become used to climbing onto Tom's lap, the better to pay attention and not miss a word of advice. Also, such close contact assured him that Mr. Gage would be paying very close attention to his version of the story!

On this particular afternoon, David assumed business as usual and promptly seated himself on Tom's lap, awaiting the principal-pupil conference. However, it seemed that this occasion called for more drastic measures, to the chagrin of the administrator, and unknown to David.

Concluding his confession, little David reached up and gave Tom a bear hug around the neck, all smiles and forgiveness, and feeling sure that the principal would reciprocate.

At this point, the teacher stated, the startled principal had to disengage David's arms and begin an explanation to the child that he was to receive a spanking. His latest transgression couldn't be settled by any other means, the teacher said.

By the time David has dismounted, bent over and Tom smacked him once on the backside, all three of them...Tom, teacher and David...were in tears!

As David pledged to act better, the incident became history...and he was hastily returned to the classroom by his shaken instructor. Patience such as this, in working with David, wasn't always a virtue of subsequent teachers or principals.

He was fortunate that his first experiences turned out as happily as they did.

More often than not, after the first grade, he was simply tolerated, rather than taught.

Sometimes the challenge of circumstances had relatively happy results: At age six, he was too young to officially be entered in the springtime Special Olympics competition, but, *nevertheless*, he was allowed to participate.

As a first grader in special education, the fact of his enrollment in the special education program was considered, rather than his IQ, making him eligible to participate. His IQ was higher than what was allowed for participants, but his teacher felt that he would benefit both from the preparations as well as from the competition.

We watched him struggle, strain, huff and puff through workouts for three sporting events.

One of the greatest results of Special Olympics is the winning spirit which is communicated to each of the participants. Hugs and pats on the back, reinforced with "Good try" and "You did great!" gave the participants the emotional and spiritual applause they so desperately need.

Southwestern Oklahoma State University students, who volunteered by adopting a handicapped athlete for the event, spent time boosting morale and encouraging each child to out-do his best. The youngsters, David among them, joyously responded.

One of our most treasured possessions was a large framed collection on his bedroom wall, containing the colorful ribbons he accumulated in two years of Special Olympics participation. Alongside was a precious picture, which still brings tears to my eyes. It showed David, in a burst of triumph, crossing the twenty-five-yard-dash line, his face wreathed in exultation, the crowd cheering and clapping.

"I knew I could…and I did it!"

We knew it, too, David!

CHAPTER THIRTEEN
Sealed School Records

In second grade, David was allowed to participate in a "normal" classroom for one hour a day, during science. This was under the guidance of a teacher who made it plain that she did not like him. David's enjoyment of the class kept him, mercifully, oblivious to her display of feelings and he always seemed to look forward to attending.

Several years later we learned, painfully, the real price he paid for having this particular teacher when we finally gained access to his previously sealed school records. We were shocked to find several notes from her, as well as comments from other former teachers, each filled with disgusting accusations and defamation. We felt, that, the presence of such material was symptomatic of the disregard those "educators" held for David.

We wondered if there were a somewhat sadistic pleasure they derived knowing that the growing stack of notes could certainly be prejudicial against David as successive teachers reviewed his files.

That second grade teacher had inserted a sheet of daily notes, covering more than a week's time, and beginning, she said, the day that David supposedly "threw a desk" at her. The incident resulted, she said, in her having a leg injury that required daily care from a chiropractor!

We found her statement difficult to believe for several reasons: Her classroom was furnished with heavy wooden desks and for all of his strength as a second grader, we doubted that David could have picked one up, much less thrown it! I couldn't pick it up!

In addition, we knew that, although he would fight like a tiger when he felt threatened, he did not, to our knowledge, initiate acts of violence. Also, what had she done to him to make him feel so threatened, if, indeed, he did hit her, with a chair? Why didn't she step aside if he shoved a chair toward her?

And, if she had been wounded as she said, why hadn't she mentioned it to the principal and to us? If there were any truth to her statement, why did she keep a list of her visits to the chiropractor and sneak them into his school file along with her unfounded accusations? Maybe she did go to the chiropractor for whatever reasons and wanted an excuse to tell her insurance company or her husband?

Her attitude was typical of those we were to encounter frequently in the next several years. We found that, teachers of "normal" children had little or no history of contact with "special" children, no idea of their needs and no desire to learn what they were.

"Special" children have an almost endless variety of mentally, physically and emotionally devastating disorders—none of which they asked for. The victims, however, and their families, must learn to endure them.

It appeared to us that the teachers, baffled by the behavior of those needful children, and inexperienced in working with such problems, had a singular unified response: "Turn your back." Exasperated, discouraged and sometimes physically aggressive to the "special" children, they appeared to assume a posture of ignoring rather than helping them.

Our attitude about the apparently uncaring teachers came not only from our personal experiences, but also from similar experiences of other parents of "special" kids with whom we shared feelings.

Of course, it would not be fair to make a judgement covering the entire field of educators. There have been many advances in special education since the time David was in elementary through high school. We realize that the teachers who years ago appeared to neither understand nor care were that way, perhaps, because of their lack of training when they were in college.

David's second year at East Elementary brought a maddeningly increasing succession of phone calls and conferences. Our veterinary practice grew busier along with the frequency of calls and I felt torn in a dozen pieces every time I heard from someone at David's school.

It seemed that almost daily there would be a complaint about him, if not from the school, then from other people. We found that, socially, his misdeeds and shortcomings were becoming topics of conversation around town! I wondered if he were the only seven-year-old in existence who had ever misbehaved! According to the stories we heard, everyone else seemed to have perfect children wonderfully mannered, academic achievers, while the Kendalls, poor things, had boys acting like children!

Presented with deteriorating situations, I tried to head for the school building and retrieve David when Tom Gage called. Sometimes, though, we were too busy for me to leave the clinic. At that point, I had to tell the unwilling-to-hear teachers to "punt" and make an extra effort to work things out with David until the school day ended.

Somehow, the problems had to be worked out, for the sake of David and everyone else.

CHAPTER FOURTEEN
What's with the Doctor?

Third grade appeared on the horizon bringing with it a renewed hope for David: An imposing man, both in academic credentials and in size, the new superintendent of schools had a Ph.D. in Special Education. For the first time we felt we would be lent a sympathetic, or at least empathetic, ear by the school administration.

"At last," we prematurely congratulated ourselves, "we will have someone on our side. He's bound to be a person who will understand and care about David and the other special students. After all, it's his field and he is bound to know about the needs of handicapped children."

Disappointment didn't wait long to find a resting-place on David's academic doorstep. The superintendent may have been *educated* to help special children but his heart did not appear to be in it. The year muddled along, following the increasingly predictable pattern of misdemeanors and punishments. One step forward, two steps backward.

We were continually dancing to a tune played by the powers-that-be. We felt that David wasn't learning because he was not being taught. Our efforts to find a solution to the problem were met with defensive accusations from the teachers. Convinced that he was capable of learning much more than he was being taught, we tried to keep the line of communication open with the school, hoping that our determination would become as important to the system as it was to us.

The end of the school year found George and me on the receiving end of a "command performance." As parents, we had been officially summoned to meet with David's various teachers plus a counselor and an apologetic Tom Gage. Out of curiosity, George's mother, Elizabeth, a dedicated teacher with more than forty years' classroom experience, attended with us.

The gist of the two-hour conference was that we were being requested…rather, told…to have David undergo even more evaluations, this time at Timberridge in Oklahoma City. "We believe that Timberridge offers fine facilities plus experienced staff members who will be helpful to all of us," said the administrators.

What they failed to say was that all payment for the expense of the requested testing would fall squarely on our shoulders. The obvious was made even more clear: We were told that if we refused to have the testing done, David would not be allowed to attend public school in Weatherford the following year. Not exactly in those words, for this was the time when civil rights issues were an especially sensitive area. George and I knew that the law provided a free public school education for all children and the public schools could not refuse David, unless they wanted to face a lawsuit.

However, the innuendoes were plain and we knew what they were telling us, without their putting it into specific words. Unless we complied with their requests, David's schooling could simply dwindle into nothingness. This was long before home schooling, which would become popular in several years and we saw no alternative.

Given such an ultimatum, we meekly complied.

The pre-evaluation procedure was familiar: Complete many forms, answer the same questions, and repeat David's background for the umpteenth time. I carefully noted anything I could recall that might seem important to the evaluator.

I paid particular attention to detail and accuracy which, I reasoned, would pave the way and prevent having to answer the same questions yet again, in person.

It was good effort on my part and might have worked, if the evaluator had bothered to look at the pages of material that I submitted!

Apparently, the "evaluator/director" didn't feel that the information which her organization had requested was worthy of her time.

When we appeared at Timberridge for the testing session, she proceeded to ask the very same questions that I had already answered on their own forms. As she quizzed me, I could see that she held the unread answers in her hand!

Dubious feelings crept into my thoughts, as an "examiner" was introduced. Her initial comment was, "I have no idea why you are here."

I explained that we had been sent by the Weatherford school system. Also, I reminded her that I had already completed and mailed the numerous forms to her office. "Did you receive them?"

Looking embarrassed and slightly confused, she replied, "Wel-l-l-l...yes, I suppose I did get them. But, I'm a very busy person and I have not had time to look them over. Just take these forms and complete them, then I'll take a look at your child."

Excusing herself, she disappeared into her office as I tried to complete the forms, balancing them atop a book on my knees.

Interrupted by a bored David, I had trouble concentrating on my answers, but after an hour had passed I felt that I had done all of the justice I could muster, to the quizzing. As I handed the completed sheets to the receptionist, she commented, "Ah, yes. Very good. Have a chair and we'll see you in a little while."

Sure you will! How "little" is the "while"?

Our appointment was at 9:00 a.m., I had been up since 5:00, just getting us ready and driving eighty-five miles, trying to get there on time. Now, it was nearly 11:00 a.m., David was tired and probably would not do well with any kind of testing...the whole situation seemed pointless...

I picked up a dog-eared magazine and gazed at the colorful pages, watching David out of the corner of my eye. He paraded around the room for the zillionth time, surveying all of the furnishings and curiously fingering the few toys which were supposed to entertain him during our enforced waiting period. At last, he settled with a puzzle and a book, just about the time the receptionist reappeared, with several instructions.

"How about making an appointment for another time?"

"Are you kidding?"

"No." She wasn't kidding.

The doctor was very busy that day and "wanted to see David some other time."

Only thinly disguising my disgust, I reminded the young woman that this appointment had originally been made with time and date set by the doctor/evaluator/director herself!

I couldn't afford to make another trip simply at the doctor's whim. "Obviously, the doctor has not taken time to familiarize herself with my son's records," I told her. She walked back toward the doctor's office.

Minutes passed. The doctor reappeared, ignoring me, motioning for David to follow her. I was told that she "has changed her mind and will proceed with his evaluation."

As they disappeared into her office, she turned, dismissing me with, "Come back after a while. We'll be busy for about two hours."

I walked to the car, sat down…prayed…and thought. Hope tentatively began to search for a footing. Surely, this would be the time and she would give us some insight into the cause and variety of David's problems. I even believed that she would help us to make plans about what to do next to help him.

Window shopping for a few minutes, I couldn't concentrate on the lovely spring fashions and the latest in home furnishings. Our budget was in its usual state of near-terminal poverty and we were facing an expensive move in a couple of months. Besides, my thoughts were riveted on what was going on at the evaluation center. Returning to the center, I waited.

Fitfully hoped.

And prayed.

I formulated numerous plans. Discarded them all.

Wonder what great, new ideas she'll have? Certainly, they're bound to be helpful. She's supposed to be experienced in testing and working with handicapped children and must know all kinds of ways to help them…

David returned to the reception area much sooner than I expected. My amazement quickly turned to frustration, then to anger, as the doctor announced that, "Everything was inconclusive."

"Inconclusive? What do you mean?"

As if speaking to a person whose comprehension was sub-par, she said slowly, and in elementary syllables, "It means, Mrs. Kendall, that I do not know what his problem is! I do not know what he needs. I cannot help you…unless you want to bring him back again, for more testing."

Of course. More testing. Why couldn't I have thought of that?

"How often? And, what are your fees?"

"Talk to the receptionist. She'll help you. I'm busy!"

Translation: I believe that my time is extremely valuable, therefore it is very expensive and I don't care to discuss dollars with you. That's why I have someone else to do the Financial talking for me. Rooted in place and disbelieving, I watched her vanish once again into her "busy," unoccupied-by-a-patient office.

David was jumping up and down, as usual, wanting to "go home…go buy ice cream…let's hurry, Mom!"

"Just a minute, son. We need to talk to the receptionist and find out about more tests. Maybe the doctor didn't get everything done today."

Although I was discouraged, I was still hopeful. It took about thirty seconds for the receptionist to administer the *coup de grace*: "You can come back in a couple of months. Call me for an appointment in about six weeks. Here's your bill for today." Smiling, she placed a sealed envelope in my hand.

I opened it and stared at the figures.

Surely, they were wrong. Maybe a misplaced decimal, or something.

Two hundred and fifty dollars!

For what?

I'd practically had to have a fit to get the doctor to even say hello to him!

True, she did have him in her office for a few minutes…but how much was her hourly rate, for crying out loud! This was 1977 and I'd never heard of anything that was so outrageously expensive as the statement I was holding. Inflation gnaws at everything, most of the time, but at that day and time, her fees were high even for her profession. Actually, hers was beginning to bear more than a passing resemblance to the Oldest Profession!

I tucked the statement into my purse, took David by the hand and left the building. There was no point in discussing either David's future testing or the excessive amount of the fee, because I felt there was little I could do about either, at that moment.

I couldn't help thinking, *Too bad she couldn't have been as inconclusive about her fee!* And, *How much longer will we be forced to participate in these charades? After all, the school wanted us to come to this place. It wasn't our choice…*

I quickly wiped aside the tears that started cascading down my face. I concentrated on David's eager recitation about his time with the doctor.

He bubbled enthusiastically during the entire ride home, answering my questions about Timberridge.

"What did you and the doctor do?"

"Wel-l-l, she read a book to me, then she asked me to color in another book."

"Did your two talk about anything?"

"Oh, yeah. Lotsa stuff. Know what?"

"No, son, what?"

"I don't think I had a good time."

"Really?"

"Yeah. She wasn't too friendly..." David's sentence trailed into nothingness as he recalled the testing and tried to put his feelings into words. "I don't think she liked me very much."

"That's too bad, son. You're a nice little boy and I think she should have liked you!"

He sadly drawled, "Wel-l-l, she didn't like me!"

His evaluation marked the end of our contact with Timberridge. *Sort of* the end of our contact, anyhow. When I withheld payment for her services, the doctor sent a brief, explicitly threatening note denying that she owed us either the oral or written diagnosis that I had requested. However, she had no difficulty making her opinion of us quite clear!

The feeling was mutual.

We offered partial payment for what we considered to have been partial (or no) help and she returned our check with another very unprofessional note attached.

We chalked up the situation to another experience, ranking this one in a special category of "The World's Highest-Priced Child Caretaker for Twenty Minutes."

The curious conclusion was that the school system never asked for results of either the testing or evaluation. We could have saved time and trouble had we never succumbed to the school's demands.

Not surprisingly, we discovered that the doctor actually was a relative of one of the persons who demanded the evaluation! Keeping everything in the family, no doubt!

We did make a point of asking some of the people who ordered us to go to Timberridge if they cared to pay the doctor's fee of $250.

They weren't interested.

Neither were we!

CHAPTER FIFTEEN
Good Friday and Other Close Calls

David's school wasn't the only chaotic area of our family life. As the veterinary practice expanded, so did working hours, leaving little time for relaxation. We remained unable to afford employees, so we spent long hours trying to just get caught up.

We would have dinner with John and David then go back up the hill to the hospital. Frequently we finished the last surgery about 9:00 p.m. George would wearily wait in the reception room, or sit on a stool in the lab, recalling the day's cases and discussing them with me as I washed instruments and made up surgical packs for the autoclave.

Homework was done under our watchful eyes at the hospital. They did schoolwork in George's sparsely furnished small office where they often played on weekends. Local restaurants became more familiar to us than our kitchen, when minutes grew too short for me to manage at the hospital and still cook at home.

Since our veterinary hospital was located up an incline, we had an excellent view of traffic in and out of the single road past the mobile home. The location also provided a panorama of the small city of Weatherford.

A mile south of town, we enjoyed the spaciousness of our surroundings. Sometimes, the wide open, treeless acres could look bleak, but more often we accepted them as they were and enjoyed the changing seasons of glorious sunrises, cloudless days and brilliant sunsets. (Of course, there was the unrelenting wind…but that's a different story.)

We felt reassured by such beauty, which would appear so suddenly on our stark landscape and then change as rapidly as it had arrived. This did not happen by accident. After unexpected rains, the wildflowers of western Oklahoma would erupt, dazzling our eyes as well as our spirits, then quickly retreat before the hot summer breezes…leaving their own special memories and promises to return.

In much the same way and with perceptible warning, we were jolted on several occasions…Not strongly enough to damage us, but certainly hard enough to remind us that God was not only still in charge but that He was closely watching over us.

Two situations etched themselves indelibly in our memories. At the time they occurred, our emotions were temporarily crushed, forcing us to discover resources within ourselves that we didn't dream existed.

Good Friday, 1975. David and I were leaving the clinic at closing time for a change, while George and John finished routine chores. Six-going-on-seven-year-olds seldom sit still, and David certainly was no exception. He'd been cautioned, as had John, to always fasten his seat belt, no matter how short a distance we were going. I assumed he'd done as expected after he climbed onto the front seat.

He didn't!

As I turned the key in the ignition, my mind was on several things that had occurred during the day. Slowly, I backed, looking over my left shoulder, turning the car around, preoccupied with the day's activities.

Suddenly, the quiet was shattered by a chilling, desperate scream from David!

My head snapped to the right. Horrified, I saw that he was no longer on the front seat. The door was open while the car was still slowly moving in reverse.

Staring at the empty seat, my eyes caught a glimpse through the windshield of my child's frenzied contortions as he wildly tossed his head and arms…he was barely visible by the right front fender.

Again, the blood curdling shriek…and then I felt a jolt and simultaneously heard a sickening "thud." Fear paralyzed me for an instant. I knew the tire had run over him!

Silence!

No more sounds of his cries.

There was only the noise of the engine, still running. I frantically grabbed the gear shift and threw it into park, terrified that the car had stopped on top of him!

"God, this can't be happening…it's a nightmare…make me wake up!"

Silently, a prayer surfaced, alongside the screams inside of me that couldn't find release through my constricted throat. I was fighting to get out of the car and my body seemed to be in slow motion. Only seconds had passed since I heard the first scream and already it seemed like forever.

Scrambling, stumbling and finally, half-falling out of the car, I found my voice.

"George! Hurry! George! Hel-l-l-l-lp!" I yelled at the top of my voice. I thought that my husband and John were on the far side of the clinic, inside, and it would have been difficult for them to hear a big truck outside, much less my cries for help.

The absolute terror in my voice penetrated the walls. George had been near a window and was watching us leave. Hearing my voice, he raced toward the car just as I knelt beside our child.

"What happened? Why is he on the ground? Did he fall?" A dozen questions tumbled from him as he tried to make sense of the scene.

Too frightened and sick to answer, I simply burst into tears, feeling for David's pulse and chest movements. George gently slipped his hand under David's neck and hollered at John who'd come running at the sound of trouble, to bring him a stethoscope. Fast!

At our touch, David sat up. And yelled, at the highest volume and most complete range he could produce.

"What happened?" George and John's duet seemed unending.

"I don't know…I don't know. He was in the car…I was backing up…"

"Fast? Were you going fast?"

"No!"

"How'd he get out of the car?"

"I don't know…just look at him and see how badly he's hurt."

When he sat up I felt somewhat relieved…at least he could move his upper torso and arms. But, where had the wheel hit him? Obviously, his head and chest didn't look bruised or bloody, but what about his legs? What if he had fragmented bones in his legs…spinal damage…smashed knees?

The expression on George's face told me that he shared my unspoken fears. We stared at the ominous dusty tire marks easily visible across David's jeans. They made a path between his knees and ankles.

"Let's go!"

George gently lifted our screaming son into his arms and dashed for the x-ray room in the clinic. I ran alongside, trying to calm a hysterical David and a badly scared John.

"Well, we'll see in a few minutes how much damage there is," George commented as he headed for the dark room.

David hadn't moved his legs voluntarily since the accident but his lungs were in perfect order. Gradually, waiting for the x-rays to develop, he became calmer. As he quieted, so did John and the pounding of my heart began to slow.

Efficiently, George placed the x-rays on the view box, ready to see exactly how terrible David's condition might be.

"I don't believe it. Look at this. Both legs!"

"Dear Lord," I prayed, "are both legs broken?"

"Carolyn, can you believe this? Not a fracture anywhere!"

No, I could not believe it, but the results were quite plain: no fractures!

In one motion, we turned to look at David's legs, again. Matching the tire marks on his jeans to the scraped places on his legs, which could have been seriously injured, we saw no bruises or abrasions.

Our son had just been run over by a very heavy car and didn't have a single scratch on him!

Over and over I'd been praying, along with George, "Please, Lord, he's already had more than enough to deal with. He's so young. How can he face another major problem?"

The Lord had an excellent answer for us.

There *was* no major problem for David!

In less than thirty minutes, he was on his feet, running through our home as though nothing had happened. The only residual effect was his hesitancy for a few weeks to climb into any car without commenting to the driver, "Please don't run over me!" This was combined with his renewed efforts to be certain his seat belt was always fastened!

It was a miracle! The weighty automobile ran over him, on a hard surface and there was almost no damage to his small body. Our miracle did not go unnoticed as we shared the story time and again with our friends and family. Their disbelief, mingled with gratitude, matched ours. Our hearts were overwhelmed.

Later, as we discussed the accident, George and I recalled a startlingly similar mishap a year earlier, which had ended tragically. A friend of ours was backing out of her driveway at noontime to pick up her husband for lunch. Her young son was in the front seat, "going after Daddy." It was Good Friday. They were only making a short trip and the child didn't fasten his seat belt.

The four-year-old yanked open the door of the slowly moving vehicle—for reasons no one will ever know—and, still clinging to the handle the way that David did, followed the outward-arching door. That was exactly what David had done when he thought the door wasn't shut…he opened it to close it tighter…and fell out, instead.

The child plunged through the vacant space as the door lazily pushed toward the front of the car, while his mother frantically tried to stop. When her car halted, it was on top of her son's chest!

I recalled how I felt, standing by the small casket, staring in disbelief at the sweet young face…so recently smiling and carefree. His angelic blond hair was carefully combed into place and his chubby little hands clutched his "most favorite" toy: a green car—exactly like Mommy's!

We shed many tears of thanksgiving that our son had been spared.

"Thank you, Lord, for saving David's life. You didn't even spare your own Son…thank you for that, too," we prayed as sleep finally quieted our household.

It seemed that he had barely recovered from his encounter with our car when David had another close call.

The cold of late winter was hanging on longer than usual for that part of Oklahoma. Snow, which usually melted rapidly, stayed on the ground for weeks, turning dingy beige as the ever-present dust from the fields settled on it.

I found getting from one place to another tougher than normal, because I had spent almost six weeks hobbling on crutches, recuperating from a badly damaged ankle. My own accident hadn't given me a vacation, though, as I continued to be at work, crutches and all, every day.

Life moved along.

George's practice was mixed, meaning that he not only had cats and dogs as patients, but he also worked on a variety of cattle, horses, sheep, etc.

It was a wintry afternoon, with George twenty miles away on a farm call for a cow in labor, when the latest near-tragedy skirted past David.

The situation could not have occurred at a worse time, as snow and ice made my crutch-supported locomotion difficult. For George, getting up the hill to the clinic in the pickup, and out on farm calls, across the icy roads, was hazardous. For me, afoot, fighting snow and crutches, it was a nightmare. I had decided that it was too much trouble climbing in and out of a vehicle with the crutches, so I walked.

Closing time approached and I dreaded the walk down the hill. An hour earlier, John had headed a half-mile across the empty wheat field to the home of a friend, with instructions to be home before dark. He promised, and took off, trailed briefly by a wailing David, who wanted to go along. John promptly returned David to the clinic, not once but twice, and I put the protesting child in the office to play, while I completed my day's bookwork.

As I finished, I called to David. No answer.

Called again. Louder. Still no response.

David was nowhere to be found, indoors or out.

Dusk was touching the skies. My mothering instincts told me that both children needed to be home, soon.

I remembered how much David had wanted to accompany John, so I immediately called to see if he had, indeed, found his way to the friend's home.

"No, he's not here."

The words sent darts through my heart.

John hurried home to help search for his brother.

I had gathered my coat and crutches and started across the darkening field to meet John. After bogging down at every step, I abandoned the effort and waited for him outside the clinic.

George still hadn't returned and there was no answer at the farm where he was working. This was still before cell phones were available…I knew it often took a while to persuade a calf to come into the world without having to do a caesarian section in the cold outdoors on a too-small/early-bred heifer. It might be hours before he returned.

John ran to the trailer. Maybe David had gone there to soothe his miffed feelings when he was left behind.

"Surely, that's where he is, and he just can't hear me when I call him and he knows he's not to answer the phone," I told myself.

"No, Mom, he's not there. I even looked in the closets and under the beds! Where is he?"

Unable to answer my son's question, I picked up the phone. It was time to ask for help. Very soon it would be pitch-black outside. Long shadows were creeping across the whitened fields. I felt a chill that had nothing to do with the weather.

I put the phone down. "No sense in bothering other people. We'll just look again, outside."

John headed in one direction and I started in another.

It rapidly became obvious that we were getting nowhere. Literally. My crutches mired in a mixture of thawing snow and red earth. Tenaciously, they refused to budge.

"So much for that. I'll call the police."

As we walked through the door, young John echoed my thoughts.

"Mom, I don't think we're gonna find him before dark. Why don't you call someone?"

Two rings and the police dispatcher answered. I tried to remain calm as I told him about my missing child.

He broke into my explanation, saying, "I'm sorry, but you're outside city limits. The police department doesn't make calls out there. Try the sheriff's office!"

Outside the city limit? Maybe by a block! How could that be? Were a few feet going to be the difference between getting help and not getting it?

Panic set in!

I hung up and told John what had happened.

Tears welled up in his eyes and he put his arms around me.

I felt shrinking confidence in my ability to get help, but I couldn't let John know.

"Don't worry, son, we'll find him soon. I'll just call the Sheriff's office and they'll help us. I'm sure they'll know exactly what to do."

I sounded more confident than I felt, as I reached for the phone, again.

Before I could pick it up, it rang.

I grabbed it, thinking, *He's at someone's house and he's alright,* not wanting to remember that the closest neighbors were at least a half-mile away. And the shadows marching across the lawn were growing longer.

A breeze started. It was going to be a very cold night.

My child was missing. Lost and alone, somewhere in the approaching darkness.

"Kendall Veterinary Clinic," I automatically answered.

"Mrs. Kendall, this is the police dispatcher."

Apparently, my frightened voice had alerted him.

"I'm sorry...I really didn't understand your problem. Help is on the way."

As, indeed, it was, for at that moment an entourage of emergency vehicles was parading up our drive toward the clinic.

They made an impressive entrance. There was the rescue unit, a van with flashing lights, in the lead, followed by an ambulance and a half-dozen automobiles, filled with volunteer personnel from the fire and rescue departments.

They piled into the clinic, spouting the expected questions: "What was he wearing? How tall is he? Hair color, weight?"

As I pulled David's picture from my billfold, I felt a lump forming in my throat. I realized that I'd seen parents on TV going through the same motions…children missing and sometimes never found…sometimes found alive and injured…Oh, God, sometimes found dead…

Lord, it's me…again. Please help these men to find David. Watch over our son…protect him until they find him. My plea was silent, unheard except by the Spirit to whom it was said.

"Yeah, I know him. Nice little kid. Was with his class last week at the fire station."

"So that's David. Sure, I know him…likes to talk."

As his picture was passed around, several rescue workers recognized him. I was surprised, for the volunteers were all strangers to me.

Quickly, several explained that they'd met him on field trips, or simply encountered him at the post office or grocery store with his dad. His naturally open, friendly manner had impressed them.

They dispersed into the dark, instructing me to stay at the clinic in case David should wander home.

John went to the trailer, still looking along the way for his little brother.

We waited. Five minutes passed, then ten, then I stopped looking at the clock.

It was quite dark. Colder winds began to move the tree branches, scratching a lonely rhythm on the clinic roof.

Moving lights caught my attention and I turned to see George parking his pickup. He rushed through the door, puzzled by all of the activity. Tears rolled down our faces as I told him what had happened.

He dashed outside, flung open the pickup door and jumped inside. Stopping at the trailer just long enough to get John, they headed down the road.

Fifteen then twenty and thirty agonizing minutes passed. Again I forced myself to leave the clock alone.

No David.

The rescuers came back and dejectedly told me they had looked everywhere they could think to search and would try again in the morning.

I watched the last of their headlights disappear into the darkness and went back to waiting and praying. "NOOOOoooooooooooooooooo! Oh, No! Tomorrow? It's cold and dark…and he's all alone…" The thoughts caught me off guard and I started to cry—again.

The rescue crew was gone. However, George would not give up so easily! He and John came back to the clinic, abandoned the pickup and left on foot with the flashlight.

Another quarter hour passed The doors flew open and in tumbled three people: George, John and an extremely muddy, tired, David!

"Thank God, he's home!"

Eagerly, George and John recounted their heroics: They had driven slowly up and down the country road between our home and town with their windows down, calling David's name and heard nothing.

Grabbing flashlights, they then headed on foot through muddy, plowed ground. Sloshing across puddles and dead grass, they tracked him by his muddy footprints leading from the clinic to the canyon. As George neared the canyon, he was calling out, "David! David!" Then, came the reply he was wanting to hear, "Here I am, Daddy!"

Finally, a pinpoint beam of George's flashlight caught something…a mud-caked, thrashing child, imprisoned by the steep walls of the narrow canyon which had held him captive for several hours.

David had apparently been hollering, unheard, for a very long time. He could see the reflections of car lights on the road, but couldn't get anyone's attention. He was nearing exhaustion. The oncoming darkness, however, boosted his adrenaline. He continued yelling out of fear of what creatures might come after him when he could no longer see his surroundings.

Our child, concerned about the increasing amount of sticky mud clinging to his boots, had removed them. He was walking in his socks through the mud, carrying his boots

He had spent time falling and sliding around, trying to get out of the canyon. In this process, his jeans and heavy coat were unbelievably covered with thick mud.

His frightened calls for help prompted George, who had skidded down the slick, straight-sided ravine walls, to move even faster. David's increasing anxiety was apparent as he cried for help. He didn't know that it was his dad, who was drawing closer.

At last! David, hoarse and frightened, allowed George to boost him to freedom, with John grabbing David's hands and tugging for all he was worth.

Finally free of his captivity, David again noticed the continuing serenade of numerous coyotes that lived nearby. They had sounded close enough to pique David's imagination. He had been seriously considering his possible fate of becoming their next meal!

"Daddy, I was so-o-o scared," he cried as he threw his arms around George. "I knew you wouldn't leave me out here, but I was so scared you'd never get here! I knew you'd come!"

Childlike faith!

What a wonderful sight—the three of them!

After numerous scrubbings, and in clean pajamas, David told his story: "I wanted to go with John…'member? I tried to follow him, 'cross the field…you had to go to the back of the clinic…and I left…He went that way…" Pointing generally in all directions, it was clear that he had no idea which way he should have gone, neither did he know which direction he actually went.

"I wanted to play, too…Then I got all lost…I fell down…I kept falling down, until," he paused, remembering, "then I slid way down far in that hole, and," he gulped, "I couldn't get out!"

Reliving the dramatic scene brought big tears to his eyes.

"I was so scared. It got real dark. I yelled and I yelled and I yelled. Nobody heard me. Nobody helped me!"

His voice was rising and tears were running in a stream down his cheeks, as he recalled his terror. Then he shrugged his shoulders, as if in defeat, repeating several times, "Nobody came…nobody got me."

"Son, I came." George was holding David on his lap as he, John and I listened to the scary tale.

"You said you knew I'd come. I wouldn't have quit looking for you…not ever."

No more explanations were needed as David reached once more for his daddy's neck, hugging him and burying his head on dad's shoulder.

What a happy ending to a situation that could have been tragic…

Another situation at Weatherford again left us wondering…about backgrounds…connections…and attitudes.

When David was a first-grader, he talked so much, after discovering speech and after his first several years in therapy that his uncle, John Paul Kendall, affectionately dubbed him "Radio." We were so thrilled to have him talking, that we constantly adjusted our conversations to include his interruptions.

However, the college student/school bus driver apparently didn't share our enthusiasm about Dave's talking. We were made aware of the bus driver's abuse when two neighboring high school girls told us that during the time that John was playing ball after school and David was riding home alone, the driver was forcing David to sit on the heater because of his talking! When his bottom started burning, he, of course, stood up! At that point, the young driver would hit David on the head with his heavy class ring, to force him to sit back down!

We reported this abuse to the superintendent and were told by him, that, "The bus driver is the nephew of a college professor and would not hurt David."

No action was taken; however, the girls watched out for David, and there were no further problems.

CHAPTER SIXTEEN
And, Then, There's New Mexico...

From late summer 1976 throughout the winter, George and I were on the road between Weatherford and Oklahoma City almost more than we were at the clinic. We both felt that if George were to successfully practice veterinary medicine, it would have to be some place other than the thinly-populated western Oklahoma county where we had located.

He stayed busy most days, but the small fees hardly made it worth his time and diligent efforts. Many long, lonely hours evaporated into yesterdays as he traveled on farm calls delivering stubborn foals, calves, piglets and lambs. More often than not, he sympathetically reduced his already-meager fees, recalling first-hand from his childhood the low profitability in farming, dairying and ranching. He knew that most of his clients simply could not afford to pay what his services were worth, but they still needed his professional care for their animals.

And, after all, he had taken an oath to alleviate animal suffering...an oath that failed to tell us who would pay the bills!

At the approach of autumn, we shared our anxieties about confronting poverty. As impossible as we imagined it would be, things really could get much worse. We had been able, by extremely carefully watching our finances, to always pay our debts. There was frequently a near-zero balance in our bank account, so luxuries were non-existent.

During the years at OSU, we had looked forward to a day of being able to afford the things we previously denied not only ourselves but also our sons. That didn't seem to be happening even after three and a half years in practice.

Common sense told us that we weren't married to the place, but to each other. If we couldn't get a better return on the investment in education, as well as our investment in the land and clinic, then we should look elsewhere to practice.

That seemed simple enough, so we started looking for a place to build a dog and cat practice. Seventy-five miles to the east, Oklahoma City seemed a likely prospect, especially the northwest quarter of the growing area.

It was soon obvious that possible building sites were over-priced and construction costs were appalling. Getting approval of the zoning commission would be daunting. Single-mindedly, though, we wasted months looking at properties, hunting for a bargain that we might be able to afford.

Our feelings of apprehension grew. If we didn't find something, what would we do? We couldn't keep existing as we were, and even hope to provide education for our sons. Sometimes, we couldn't even afford clothes and shoes!

Christmas passed…suddenly it was Valentine's Day…and still nothing. We looked, but nothing was available that our small budget could afford for a down payment. We needed help!

One evening in late February, George and I realized that, once again, we had approached a situation all wrong, for in all of our months of searching, we had not really ever asked God what He had in mind for us!

Together, we prayed, asking God to give us the guidance we needed to find the right place. More than that, we prayed for the wisdom to recognize His answer when it came. "God, we give up…we can't do it…and we turn it over to You…and just wait for Your answer!" Then, we had peace of mind about it.

A couple of nights later, George was reading a journal which listed the board exams and testing dates for a number of states. He suddenly called to me in the kitchen, "Hey! Look at this! Would you believe that Frankie Elliot is the executive secretary of the New Mexico Board of Examiners?"

That's nice, I thought, as I recalled Dr. Elliot from OSU. Both she and her husband were veterinarians and instructors. They had moved to Santa Fe where they had a pet practice. She had been a wonderfully friendly lady, kind to us student-wives, and I immediately remembered her.

"What about it?" I wondered aloud to George.

"Well, what do you think about me making a phone call to her? Maybe she'd know of someone looking for an associate…maybe even a practice for sale in New Mexico."

Practice for sale? I visualized our most recent paltry bank statement and smiled.

"Sure, why not? Couldn't hurt to ask."

Fifteen minutes later, hanging up the phone, my husband was all smiles. "She said that she's just getting ready to have the quarterly newsletter printed and she'll put in a notice that I'm looking for a place," he announced.

New Mexico?

Seriously?

George did not have a license to practice there, and perish the thought of taking a fourth board exam! The tough national test, plus licensing exams for Oklahoma and Arkansas had almost physically polished him off when he graduated three years earlier. To consider doing it again was worrisome.

I couldn't let him see how deeply I was concerned, so I tried to sound encouraging.

"Yes, maybe there will be a place for us, out there on the desert."

Two weeks later, we received a phone call from a doctor in the well-known "alien city" of Roswell, New Mexico. He said that he needed an associate and invited us to visit. George accepted the invitation.

Three nights before our anticipated trip, there was another phone call, from a doctor in Clovis, New Mexico who had his practice and home for sale. George told him we'd already planned to drive through Clovis, so of course we'd take a look.

We speculated the entire 300 miles from Weatherford to Clovis about what we might find. We already knew that no matter where we practiced, if George owned the place I would have to work in the practice and our home would need to be close by. Very close.

We had been told that the Clovis practice had a home right next door, which sounded hopeful, although we couldn't imagine such a ready-made solution to our needs. When we arrived late on Friday, we took a quick tour of the large clinic and the home. Surprised and pleased about the property, we were told that after down payment the doctor and his wife would carry the balance at seven percent, which in 1977 was a fair amount.

We were told that several other practitioners were interested in and considering the property. We had no way of knowing if the clinic and home would even be available when we returned.

Again, we asked God for help in our decision making.

He did!

During the Roswell visit, anxious feelings began to creep into the glances that George and I exchanged. Somehow, the situation didn't seem right and we felt that this was not the place for George.

Very late Sunday evening we were back in Clovis at the home of my cousin (we couldn't afford a motel), discussing finances, licensing exams, etc. How, in fact, could we commit ourselves to New Mexico when George didn't have a license for that state?

Equally as much a concern was the fact that we didn't even have enough money for the down payment!

In fact, we didn't know if it were still for sale or had already been sold...

Before George called early Monday to find out if the property were still available, we agreed to accept whatever answer the phone call would bring.

For as long as I live, I will be able to see the expression on George's face as he talked: "Yes, this is George Kendall. Carolyn and I were wondering if you've already sold the clinic."

Silence, as George listened.

For fully two minutes he listened, saying nothing, just nodding.

He turned his back to me and I felt my hopes sinking.

"I'll just bet they've already sold it," I turned to my waiting relatives and softly commented.

Suddenly, George's voice became animated and I heard him saying, "Do you mean it?"

I turned and faced him, and the smile on his face said it all: The clinic and the home would be ours!

Our decision was made!

God's plan could not have been more obvious if a lightening bolt had come down from Heaven! The owner, Dr. Ben Russell, told George, "My wife and I would rather sell to you and Carolyn. We decided that if you really want to buy, we'll carry the balance for six percent instead of the seven percent we were asking!"

"Yes, of course we want to buy!"

George could hardly get the words out fast enough, turning his beaming face in my direction.

Six days later, after a speedy thousand miles back and forth from Weatherford to Clovis to our attorney in my hometown, George had the contract signed and our down payment in sight.

"Even if we don't have all of the money for the down payment today, we know we'll have it by the time it's due," we had optimistically decided…and, sure enough, we sold some of our acreage at Weatherford just in time to meet the deadline.

We knew that George could not practice until he passed the state licensing exams that were still more than two months away. We convinced ourselves that our decision was right and he would pass.

On this faith, we immediately started moving. My relatives generously offered storage and after weeks of traipsing back and forth, we had the move well underway.

Exam time arrived in early June and George spent three days in Albuquerque undergoing the rigors of becoming licensed in New Mexico. Exhausted, he arrived home late Wednesday, saying that the instructions to the candidates were, "Don't call the board, you'll know if you passed the exams when you receive your license in the mail. It may take ten days to two weeks."

His license was in the noon mail on Friday!

One hurdle passed, more arriving. A visit with the assistant superintendent of schools at Clovis assured us that there would be the right educational opportunities for both John and David.

Our older son, entering sixth grade, had spent the preceding two years in a gifted class at Weatherford, his eager mind stimulated and challenged by a variety of programs not available in the regular classroom.

David, in his ungraded special education classroom, was ready for new horizons, also.

We were repeatedly advised that both would be placed in proper settings and, indeed, that such classes were already available.

Wrong!

Enrolment time arrived in the tormenting heat of New Mexico in mid-August.

Off we went…to find that the school that our boys should be attending had absolutely nothing to offer either special ed or gifted children.

Disappointed, and wondering what could happen next, George and I spent several days discussing what we should do. We were in the midst of a particularly trying time with David, who was dissatisfied and upset by the move from Weatherford. Predictably, he was having adjustment difficulties.

One especially upsetting afternoon, when it seemed impossible to reach David, who was doing everything he could to be disagreeable, I remembered an advertisement I'd heard a few days earlier on TV. It pointed out that in Victoria, Texas, there was a boarding school for handicapped children that supposedly offered many types of help both for the youngsters as well as for their families.

I felt the usual pressure and apparently had no alternative, so I called the school. By the time the registrar answered, I was in absolute disarray...in tears and hardly coherent. Patiently, he listened, while I haltingly tried to tell him about David, punctuating my sentences with tearful outbursts.

When I paused, he'd quietly ask questions, then wait for answers. He'd been exposed to this situation numerous times and his approach was to be a kindhearted, sympathetic listener. What a welcome relief from the defensive position professionals had placed me in on other occasions!

As we closed the conversation, he promised to send literature to answer questions. It arrived forty-eight hours later. When we saw pictures of the school and read of their work, we felt briefly hopeful. However, when we reached the tuition information, our hopes evaporated. There was no way we could afford to send David to that, or any other of several private schools which I'd recently contacted.

The answer to the problem was that he would have to go to school in Clovis.

So would John.

Scrambling around at the last minute, we were sent by the school administration to enroll David in a special ed class at Bickley School. John, with some encouragement from us and his newly found friends agreed to go to Zia Elementary. We soon found that neither child was receiving what we considered to be even barely adequate teaching.

David roughed it, literally, until the end of the school year, one step forward and three steps in reverse. At first we were amazed, then disgusted, with the notes he brought home from the teacher. We wondered how she had managed to complete college because of the interesting grammar and spelling in her communications. When I forwarded a collection of her notes to the superintendent, I never received a reply from him.

And, of course, the teacher resented my intrusion into her professional life. Her feelings didn't bother me, as I was concerned only about how she could be teaching grammar and spelling when she used them so poorly herself. The only changes in her notes about David were an increase in frequency and criticism.

At mid-year, we moved John to Sandia School. Out of our district but with a better teacher; perhaps his entire year would not be wasted. He would soon be entering seventh grade and needed this year to be as informed and well-taught as possible.

Football and band occupied John's extra-curricular hours, while David passed the time reading and drawing...making a world of his own where he was accepted. No peer pressure plagued him within the secure confines of his own room. There, if he did not always excel, at least he was not found lacking.

We cheered John's team from the windy sidelines during football season even as their best wasn't good enough to beat other teams.

We encouraged David's academic endeavors, although, that year, things just never jelled for our younger son, and it appeared that the harder he tried, the worse things became.

Each school year started with our permission for more testing on David, followed by his re-placement in the self-contained classroom. At what should have been the fifth grade level, he could not write cursive, could not understand the simplest math and appeared to be on high center. Reading remained the sole pleasure of his school days.

George and I made frequent trips to school to visit with teachers, speech therapists and the Director of Special Education...and got nowhere.

Often we heard, "We're doing the best that we can. He just won't sit still...and he causes so many problems in the classroom that it's hard to teach the other children."

David had been taken off the Mellaril when we moved to Clovis, as he didn't seem to need it. He had undergone a tonsillectomy at Weatherford shortly before we left there and afterward appeared to be much calmer. His self-control was more noticeable and he told us that he believed that he was able to do without the pills. Since he was the best judge of the situation, we stopped the medication.

Then, hearing the complaints, we wondered if we had done the right thing...perhaps he still needed the chemical support to help keep his hyperactive body under control. So, he took an occasional pill when he'd feel that he was in need of it, and eventually weaned himself altogether.

We wondered if our son were the entire cause of the teacher's seeming inability to instruct, as he was portrayed during conferences. We also wondered why David always appeared to be the culprit. Was there no other child in the school, much less in the special ed classroom, who caused problems?

During the school year, David continually practiced forgive and forget, two character assets that are among his outstanding traits today. Forget comes first in the dictionary and has always come first with David. It has made his process of forgiveness more meaningful.

Blessed by such a powerful foundation for his life, David has been able to, literally, blind himself to accusations, hurts and disappointments. The multitude of grief-ridden, shattering experiences that he has overcome, didn't turn him into a bitter person, although they could have.

He emerged as a gentle, sensitive, deeply caring man, able to accept the freedom to be himself and not ashamed of who or what he is.

At the tender age of ten, acceptance was difficult as unthinking adults, peers and teachers attacked him from every side, in and out of school. He was not as convinced then, as he is now, of his own worth. However, he was able to forgive himself even when other people were unforgiving of him.

To his family, this seemed a major accomplishment. It is a mark of maturity for anyone, "normal," gifted or in-between. Considered in the light of frequently unjustified accusations and recriminations against him, David's adjustment seems all the more satisfying.

We were midway through our first winter in Clovis. Blustery days juggled between hours of warm sunshine. Happily, we compared the passing season to the last several we had endured in western Oklahoma. We definitely favored the milder temperatures of New Mexico and looked forward to springtime.

There were moments, however, that temporarily halted our sunshine, as in the case of the torn coat. It began with the telephone, as usual, heralding yet another unwelcome tiding from the school principal.

Answering the phone at the clinic, I was informed that an entire week earlier, on the playground, David had ripped a teacher's coat and that "you and your husband should be prepared to buy her a new one." After the fact, he added, that we "should do this immediately."

Astounded, I asked for the name of the teacher, plus the circumstances of the incident.

"Please tell me why David is being accused and we are asked to replace her coat."

I heard a vague, unintelligible response.

"When did this happen?"

"At noon."

"Where?"

"On the playground."

136

"Why did you and the teacher wait a week to say something about this?"

"She just came to my office today to tell me."

"Oh, I see. Well, just how did this take place?"

"I don't know. I wasn't there. She said that David ran past her and pulled on the arm of her coat and it ripped and she wants a new coat."

Good for her, I said to myself. *I'd like a new coat, also, if I could get one using the same tactics.*

Of the principal, I requested that the teacher bring the torn coat to our clinic that afternoon. George and I would discuss the situation with her.

At the close of the school day, when I was facing the last of several waiting clients, sorting them into exam rooms, the teacher appeared, coat over her arm. It was a pigskin garment, obviously several years old, and well worn.

I asked her to go to an exam room to talk to my husband, who asked her to put the coat on. When she did, we noticed the extremely tight fit, even though the teacher was a very petite woman. The coat featured an inset belt, which hung only by threads, showing the effects of her countless tugs to pull it tightly at the waist.

At George's request, she stretched her arms to hug her chest and appeared to be snugly encased. Too snugly!

We asked to see the damage that she insisted had been caused by David.

She said, "Here, the seam under the sleeve. See, the sleeve is pulled loose from the rest of the coat."

Sure enough, the seams under the armpits, on *both* sides of the coat, were stretched, showing threads where there should have been a tightly sewn seam, with one of them ripped loose.

"What are you saying that he did?"

Answering, she claimed that on the schoolyard she and another teacher were talking. She said that she noticed David run past her, and she felt a bump on her arm. She admitted that she didn't know if he reached out, actually touching her arm or not; in reality, she had seen nothing.

However, "sometime later that day I noticed that the sleeve was ripped at the seam," and at that point, she stated that she "recalled that David had run past and it must have been him who caused the damage."

The logic of the statement escaped both George and me. I found it difficult to keep from laughing. She had, somehow, decided that, based on the torn, worn, sleeve, we owed her a new coat!

We were very curious: Why had she waited seven days to complain to the principal? Why did she not report the problem immediately, especially since she was now so freely accusing our son? And, why did she ask the principal to call us, rather than coming to talk to us herself?

Why did she blame David, anyway? Her coat appeared to be suffering from long-time wear and abuse. It seemed, from its apparent age and dirty condition, that it had seen better days. She admitted that she thought he'd bumped her on only one side, but seams under both sleeves were in an identically worn and pulled condition.

Adamantly, she began to insist that Dave had hit her. She then repeated her story, adding that he had grabbed her arm. Each new statement seemed to contradict her previous ones. It appeared that she was now trying to convince herself that David truly was at fault!

After a few minutes, the truth inadvertently slipped: Her husband had cautioned her to not wear that particular coat to school and, until the day of the incident in question, she said she had left it at home. That one time, she said, she wore it against his wishes, and, when he saw the condition of the sleeves, he became furious with her.

Interesting, we thought. Keep talking…

Then, the rest of the story surfaced, as she unthinkingly mentioned David's special education status. Suddenly, the situation became obvious: This teacher was blaming David (1) because he was a special ed student who had few resources with which to defend himself against her charges, and (2) he happened to be on the playground at the same time that she was. Amazingly, she admitted that the teacher to whom she was talking at the time the sleeve seam was torn didn't notice anything out of the ordinary, didn't see David touch her or her coat sleeve, didn't observe the sleeve tearing!

This young woman was aware that David would be unable to verbally defend himself against her accusations. She knew, as we did, that his history of behavior problems at school would lend credence to her charges, even if they were untrue, which they were.

She asked for $300 to replace her coat! Three hundred dollars? In 1978 dollars…for a sad looking piece of used clothing, too small for the owner and too dirty, worn and bedraggled to be used for anything?

We specifically asked our insurance company to not pay her claim. We believed that David was innocent of her charges. She had proven nothing, we felt, and that's exactly what she should receive: Nothing!

However, after our insurance company received a letter threatening legal action against the company and us, they paid $75 for repair of the garment, without telling us that they had settled with her. We accidentally found out that the claim had been paid and we were not happy about it!

After finding out, we asked to see the insurance company's files on the incident and found that even when the company quizzed her, she could not say with certainty that David had actually touched her, much less hit her or pulled on the sleeve enough to rip it.

She admitted that the damage had not been noticed until much later in the day, and, further, she agreed that if David had, indeed, jostled her while running past, there was no ulterior motive on his part.

The only guilt that our child bore was to have been in the vicinity, as were many other children. He, however, was the only one nearby who was in the handicapped class and the only child nearby whose father was a doctor (which, to some people, is synonymous with money, although not the case with us). The blame migrated to him.

It could have been interesting to discover if she ever had the useless coat repaired—but we didn't care enough to pursue it. Issue closed.

CHAPTER SEVENTEEN
Can You Believe It?

Suddenly, a new scene unfolded, or rather, a replay of the Timberridge episode, came walking into our living room. In the newest version, a school nurse assumed the starring role. She was the wife of the retirement-age Clovis superintendent of schools, and a stranger to me. The morning she selected for her first unannounced meeting was not the best time she could have chosen.

True, everything considered, our lives were moving along fairly well. It was approaching spring, March 1978. George was engrossed in his new clinical surroundings. I spent many hours working two steps behind him. John was living it up drawing admiring glances from pre-teen girls as he peddled back and forth to his school while David struggled just to survive at another school. To our distinct pleasure, financially we were beginning to see black instead of red and we remained hopeful about our newfound success in the veterinary practice.

Then, she came to visit!

When this woman unexpectedly rang our doorbell on that warm beautiful morning, I was trying to dig out from under a mound of clinic bookkeeping. I'd planned to spend a busy hour catching up, and then go to the clinic. I was not prepared to waste an hour listening to a re-hash of David's various exceptionalities. Thankfully, when I answered the ringing, I was unaware of what awaited.

The woman fairly bulldozed her way into our living room, firmly planting herself on our sofa, hastily introducing herself. Her harangue began…and continued…on and on…for sixty extremely trying minutes.

She enumerated all of David's faults of which she was keenly aware…ones that even I had forgotten. In a monologue that gripped my attention, she listed his misbehaviors, anti-social antics, various misdeeds and social sins. Her lengthy list seemed to have no end. Nor did her ability to recount his actions.

Wide-eyed and attentive, I hardly moved.

With a touch of horror, I realized that I was losing a battle with my face, to keep it under control so that I wouldn't laugh at her.

My stars, I thought, *this woman has rehearsed her tirade. She doesn't want to miss a misdemeanor!* That play on words amused me, and my facial expression reflected it, just as she increased her speed and volume!

Similar word games tumbled across one another in my mind, as I entertained myself, pretending (and, hopefully, appearing) to give her my undivided attention. I had already guessed the purpose of her visit before she mentioned it: Have David tested…or else!

Sure enough, not even pausing for a breath, she made her point, demanding our immediate attention to find a professional evaluation for Dave.

Finally, my patience and amusement wore thin. I found that the effort to remain calm was costing me dearly when realized that I had unknowingly started to clench my hands and grit my teeth. It was an effort, though not a good one, to halt the thumping that I felt rising from my chest to my head. The humor I previously felt was gone.

Taking advantage of a very brief pause in her chanting, I swallowed a couple of times, found my voice and asked, "Are you aware of all of the tests that David has undergone in his nine years?"

"Oh, yes, but we need more…with current results," she assured me. When I inquired about who "we" was, she was not able to tell me.

She plowed on. Like ghosts of Christmas Past, the specter arose again: Have The Evaluation Done. You Have No Choice. If You Don't, Then You Can Forget About David Attending Public School in Clovis.

True, she didn't use that exact threat, but she waltzed that hint past me several times.

Of course, I was aware of the law concerning public school education being provided for all children, handicapped and "normal." I felt sure that the nurse, her superintendent-husband and the school board would not enjoy being immersed in a "failure to educate" lawsuit...and, of course, neither would George, David and I!

My inclination was to shout at her.

I didn't.

A solution would be to usher her to the door and the safety of the outdoors before I lost my temper.

I ushered!

With assurances, that, "Dr. Kendall and I will talk about this," I left her at our gate and returned to my book work.

We did discuss the issue. Then we dismissed it, fervently hoping that the chapter was closed and we would not hear from it or her again.

The chapter, however, was still wide open!

A few weeks later, undaunted, the unwelcome person stalked back to our front door.

Again, unannounced...uninvited...unwanted. Skipping amenities this time, she asked, "Why haven't you had your son evaluated?"

I avoided the honest, direct answer: "We never had any intention of paying for any more unnecessary testing" and told her, instead, that we were "considering" it.

The displeasure she must have felt showed plainly across her countenance. She frowned, looking if possible even more unpleasant than before. Announcing that she would not leave our home until I told her that I would, that very day, make arrangements at Amarillo for tests, she planted herself once again on our sofa.

I considered the frightening possibility of having her stay even a few more minutes. That was enough to prompt me to commit myself to calling the evaluation center before it closed that day!

Stressed to the maximum, thoroughly irritated at this unwanted intruder, and having listened to another hour of her derogatory comments about David, I felt that she and I were both on thin ice. Thin to the cracking point...

After I promised to comply with her demands, she seemed satisfied, ceased her incantations and, mercifully, departed.

Years later, I was informed that I should have contacted the school system and the office of special education to find out exactly what was going on. However, the woman seemed so sure of herself, and of her position with the schools, so full of authority and accusations, that I assumed there were no choices: I had to do what she said; otherwise, David would be tossed out of school.

Two weeks later, Dave and I greeted a dismal, rainy April sunrise as we headed 110 miles north toward Amarillo, Texas.

My sleepy son had set up howls of protest when we awakened him at 5:00 a.m. However, by the time we drove two hours, crossed the central/mountain time zone (losing an hour), we were grateful to have gotten an early start. We arrived just barely on time for our 9:00 a.m. appointment.

David had instantaneously dropped off to sleep when he sat down in the car, and I kept myself alert, listening to the gloomy weather predictions, punctuating them with my bleak thoughts and opinions: "Two hundred miles round trip in the rain, today…maybe it will be worth it. Little else has been beneficial…keeping David out of school for another test…paying more money for no help…and I had to get up at 4:30…what a mess!"

I kept muttering to myself as another truck hauling cattle, the fifth in as many minutes, inundated us with more water—and mud.

Seven hours later and dollars poorer, we splashed homeward. We'd been given no answers. Just more questions.

And those tests! The ones that David disliked so intensely. The one, in fact, with questions he had memorized after having been subjected to them so frequently.

Memorized and often refused to answer, because his obstinacy often gained him more attention than his answers did. He had discovered a method of defensively handling the evaluation-testing program. It was difficult to blame him for his negative attitude. My own was no better. Being honest about my personal feelings, I admitted having sympathy for his barely tolerant submission to the seemingly endless barrage.

We had all begun to resent the pointless probing, quizzing and nosing around, not only in David's life, but also in our small family's.

If we had been given hope or help, undoubtedly everyone would have felt more cooperative. But, covering the same useless territory time and again, resulting only in the discouragingly predictable answers, was demoralizing.

We wanted to remain hopeful.

This newest testing didn't help erase any doubts. Neither did our vain wait for the school system to inquire about the evaluation results that were so important to the wife of the superintendent. No one ever asked! Wasted time and money, again.

Some light was shed on the situation more than a year later when I mentioned the ridiculous episode to Carolyn Luck, Director of Special Education for the Clovis School system. George and I found, to the mutual dismay of Carolyn and us, that no one—with the exception of the superintendent's wife—had wanted, asked for or required the tests!

No one.

Mrs. Luck was genuinely horrified to learn about what had taken place, and she assured me that neither she, nor anyone else, had needed, asked for nor appreciated the intrusion of that woman. It was, simply, another exercise in futility, with David paying the emotional price and with George and me being handed the financial bill.

The Saturday evening following the Amarillo tests, I heard David in his bedroom, crying and talking to himself. "Why can't I be like everyone else? What's wrong with me?"

He sobbed as if his heart were breaking.

I let him have his private moment, agonizing over what he felt were his inadequacies, trying to work out some answers for himself. After several minutes, I became alarmed. His pleadings sounded increasingly desperate.

Walking into his room, I found him face down on his damp pillow, face flushed, eyes brimming with tears and hurt, expecting me to answer the unanswerable questions.

As I took David in my arms, I asked, "Son, what's happened? Why are you crying? Has someone hurt you?"

"N-n-n-nobody's hurt me. I hurt m-m-m-myself. All the time."

He continued to shed bitter tears of frustration, "I don't know wha-a-at to do-o-o-o-o-o about it. Why do I have to be so different? Why can't I be like everyone else? Like John? Like you and Dad? Why do I have to LIVE LIKE THIS?"

His voice reached a crescendo, peaking at a level that unnerved me.

George came running into the room, surveying the scene, asking, "What's going on? It sounds like World War Three in here!"

I tried to briefly explain, over the sound of David's moans and self-battle. The child had reached the end of his emotional rope, and it frightened me.

I'd heard and read about the suicide rate among elementary-age children. The thought sickened me that we might be witnessing the symptoms in our son.

David repeated, "Why do I have to live?"

God, I prayed, *somehow, some way, give us the wisdom to share strength with*

David, to build up his emotional resources, right now! Give us the right words to ease his pain and help him. Lord, You know that we don't have any idea what to do, but You do. Help all of us!

His storm subsiding, tears drying, David put his arms around my neck and his head on my shoulder, as he had done when he was a hurt pre-schooler.

"Son, Daddy and I have done all we know to do, to help you. You know that. We hurt with you."

"We love you. We want a happy life for you," George comforted him.

"When you ask, 'Why do I have to be different,' there's only one answer that I can think of," I went on. "God made everyone different from everyone else. You know, not everyone can draw the way that you can, or sing the way that you can. Not everyone can sew or cook or be a doctor. We all have special talents that God gave us. Some people may have more talents that we admire, or else, maybe, their talents are more noticeable and we can see them better…"

"You know, sometimes, some people just go through life not using all of the neat, wonderful things that God has given them the ability to do," my husband added.

"We have no answer for you about why you were born with brain damage, or why you've had so many problems. But, we can tell you this, you can believe that you are a very special person with very wonderful talents, and you will use them someday to bring hope and help to other people," I told him, my voice shaking.

"Son, it's not bad to be different. Your dad and your brother and I are all different from each other and different from other people. Just imagine what a dull world it would be, if we were all exactly alike. We'd simply be a bunch of robots, instead of interesting people. I know you love and admire John and want to be like him and make good grades and have so many friends and fun things to do. But, it's not wrong to be different from him, because another word for different is special and unique and that's what you are!

"God must love you a bunch, to make you so noticeable. I know He has a special message for you to share with the world, and He wants people to pay attention to you and to remember you. Maybe, it's hard to understand now, especially when you want to be exactly like all of the kids at school. Just remember, though, that special people receive special blessings. Look what you have to look forward to!" I concluded, hoping that I sounded at least a little convincing.

The puzzled expression left his tear-streaked face, replaced by a small smile at first, and then by a full-blown delighted grin that seemed to say, "That helps me to accept myself a little better."

I was amazed at what George and I had just shared, and as we realized that it did not come from our own wisdom, we joined hands with David to tell God thank you for giving us such a special person in our home. And for being with us through the hard times.

CHAPTER EIGHTEEN
Conquering the Bicycle

Challenges waited around each corner, some with happy results. The warm days brought out bicycles and baseball, all accompanied by agile, eager children of all sizes and ages. David watched longingly as school children zipped up and down the streets on their two-wheelers, laughing and teasing and having fun. They were so free…so mobile!

His viewpoint from the sideline wasn't any fun at all. He was a larger-than-life nine-and-a-half year-old with such coordination problems that he still could not ride a bicycle. Frequently, when he thought no one was watching, he'd stand John's bike upright on the driveway, stare at it for long minutes, then sadly tug it around the parking lot at the clinic then return it to the front yard.

We knew how much he wanted to be able to have the mobility of his classmates…but wishing simply wasn't the answer. John and George took turns trying to hold the bike upright, with David perched on the seat, and each scenario ended with everyone sprawled on the ground.

A few sessions like that and David thanked them for their assistance, but he said he'd "rather do it by myself."

Wise child.

That bicycle silently goaded, threatened and prodded him.

Brain damage had affected his ability to maintain balance and to produce the consecutive right-left movements that are critical not only to bike riding but also to reading the English language.

His eye-hand coordination lagged far behind his physical growth. Long past the time when other kids had peddled independently into their young worlds, David was still only an observer, wishful and lonely. Discouraged and embarrassed by his inability to perform what seemed to be such a simple task, he vowed to prove that he could keep his balance and learn to ride.

Doggedly, he pursued the project. Unwavering, he worked for eight long, scarred, frequently bloody weeks.

Before and after school, he would take the two-wheeler for walks. That's all. Just grab the handlebars and stroll alongside, his face showing his deep concentration. Walking, the peddles noiselessly circling…taunting him…enticing…daring him to make them obedient to his commands!

Walking.

Slowly.

Then faster.

Eventually straddling the bike, awkwardly walking it.

More walking.

Gritting his teeth, setting his jaw.

The battle lines were drawn.

Another challenge, confronted head-on.

Literally.

Days passed.

From the windows of our home and clinic, we would glance outside, not wanting to further embarrass him. Not wanting him to know that we shared his challenge…and his agony.

"Lord, please, he's so young and has known so little success. Let him feel the excitement, know the joy of achievement…of doing something on his own. Whatever it takes, please let his young legs work right. Help him to know victory."

Days evolved into weeks. Cautiously, then bravely, he experimentally put one foot on an upraised pedal.

Push.

Coast.

Push.

Coast.

Always, there was a price to pay. Like a battle-weary warrior, he appeared at mealtimes, dotted with bruises, cuts, sweat and scrapes.

Uncomplaining.

With only one request, "Don't help me! I've got to do it myself!"

Such wisdom!

Life's that way. What we learn best, we often have to learn by hard work. No one else can experience anything in our place.

Once the knowledge or experience is ours, then it is ours for a lifetime. No one can take the achievement from us.

And, David longed for the exhilaration that comes from conquering...from daring to meet the monster, defying him and winning!

The Big Day finally arrived: With no hint of what we were to witness, no bugles playing, no drums heralding the accomplishment, he came to us, softly entering the front door and quietly requesting, "Come outside, just for a minute. I want you to see something."

Wondering if this could be it and swallowing our excitement, George and I hurried to the yard.

We watched as he pushed the bike to the street at least seventy-five feet away. Bravely, he mounted the two-wheeler. John and our cat joined us, and we became the cheering squad in front of our wooden fence.

Anxiously, we watched Dave tentatively begin his trip across the asphalt. Simultaneously gaining confidence and momentum, he peddled faster and faster.

I can still see him, zooming toward us, legs furiously in motion, his body upright and *balanced* on that blessed bicycle...

He was grinning, beaming actually, his hair ruffled by the small breeze he was stirring...

Weeks of scratches and bruises faded. Long, miserable hours vanished.

Riding! At last!

He couldn't have been more thrilled, nor could we, if he'd just completed an Olympic marathon, which indeed we felt that he had!

Not even an undignified descent, as he smashed into the fence, marred the occasion.

Sheepishly smiling at all of us, he ducked his head and admitted, "I don't know how to stop, yet. But, I will."

Yes, David, that, and so much more!

How much more? Well, slowing down wasn't always high on David's list of must-do's...as we observed to our horror after Hallowe'en.

George's mother had constructed a Batman costume for David, at his request. She had completed the blue top and pants with the yellow circle displaying a black bat in full flight. Also, a matching cape.

All went well, David paraded around the house and yard, having an excellent time trick or treating and continued to wear the outfit as pajamas.

All went well—until Christmastime. A week before Christmas, George and I left the house for about twenty minutes, dashed across the street to the mall and raced back.

When we entered the front door, on our right was the colorful Christmas tree in its full glory…and on the left was David, on top of the large wooden dining room table with a screwdriver in his hand, aiming for now-naked wires and an empty ceiling fixture where the fan and light had formerly been attached! He was clad in his favorite Batman pajamas with his cape lying suspiciously on the floor.

The ceiling fan, which was never turned off except to be cleaned, lay at his feet. In pieces. George's tool box lay open on the floor, contents strung across the carpet.

"David, what are you doing?" George and I were beyond frightened—scared silly was accurate—at the sight of our son aiming for the ceiling with the metal-bladed tool…going to not only short-out the house, but his life along with it!

"Mom and Dad, don't be mad at me, please! I was gonna fix this back. It'll be O.K."

"We're not mad…just nervous wrecks! What in the world happened?"

"Well," he began, trying to collect his thoughts as he recited the details of the "accident," "It's like this…I…uh…the fan…ummm…well, I don't know what happened."

"O.K., Dave, let's try this for starters," George and I helped him out.

"You had your cape on…your turned the fan off then you thought you'd go flying by holding onto the ceiling fan and turning it…you're too heavy for it," we told him. "And the fan and light fell down. How're we doing?"

"Yeah, that's what happened!"

"David, didn't you know that you could electrocute yourself? Sticking the screwdriver into the wires?" George was dumbfounded by what he was seeing!

"Uh, well, Dad, I didn't think about it, I guess…did I do something wrong?"

"Dave, not really…we're just very glad that you stopped trying to help before you killed yourself!"

And, do we suppose that he didn't try that again? Suppose so…

CHAPTER NINETEEN
Music, Math and Fractures

Ignoring our written opposition and against our better judgement, David was placed in special ed fifth grade at Bella Vista, an out-of-district ghetto school on the opposite side of town from our home.

In these surroundings, David had to immediately develop some street smarts including an even tougher emotional exterior than he already had. The tough guy image of Bella Vista students and teachers made us wonder about our son's physical safety. Even the youngest pupils appeared to be cautious, streetwise and a great deal more sophisticated than our son was.

However, each time we tried to discuss our apprehension with the officials, we were told that Bella Vista's special education classroom was "the only one in town for David. It's that room...or nothing! Take it or leave it!"

We took it.

Segregated from "normal" students, David rode the special ed bus and attempted to adjust to his new surroundings. It seemed as if every year he'd been in a different school with no continuity of personnel or peers.

He began to wonder, aloud, if this were his own fault...after all, if he were not at fault, why would he be shifted around so frequently? He couldn't make sense of the situation. George and I also found it difficult to understand.

Physically, he was growing at an awesome rate. Tall, rather stocky and stronger than he realized, he could have literally flattened the school yard tormentors. Dave chose, instead, to try to communicate with them.

However, talking did not work.

Weeks passed.

He began to withdraw into a small world, inhabited only by imaginary friends and real books, neither of which would cause him the pain he found so hard to bear at school.

Ragged edges formed the boundary of his life. Peer acceptance was non-existent and pressure from the so-called "normal" kids was unending. Special ed classmates added to his distress in the classroom…while teachers were openly hostile to him.

Always tall for his age, he seemed to grow even taller almost weekly. He towered above his special education teacher. The young teacher was a new graduate, inexperienced, in spite of having the master's degree required in New Mexico to teach special ed.

When George and I asked about David's progress, she seemed to be particularly disinterested, impatient and vague. Unless she was sharing information about any *mis*behaviors, she had little to say to us.

The concept of mathematics, which had been extremely difficult for him, continued to undermine his days at school. We wondered if this teacher would be able to show him how to solve even the most basic problems.

Still naive and trusting, we depended on the honesty of teachers and administrators, in order to gauge David's academic progress. Trying to keep communication open, we made frequent trips to talk to teachers, often after we ate lunch with our son in the school lunchroom.

These in-person discussions were seldom productive, as were the barrage of complaining notes and phone calls from the teacher, covering everything from David's classroom behavior and inattentiveness to "his extreme distractibility and lack of cooperation."

For his part, David was frustrated with school, resisting class work in the incomprehensible math and in cursive writing, which looked easy as he watched other students doing it. His delayed development in gross and fine motor skills slowed his eye/hand/finger coordination. Completing a written assignment was almost impossible and certain to take hours of struggle for what would have been only a few minutes for a person with cooperative fingers.

Homework frequently ended in David's personal disgust with his lack of ability to do something a "normal second grader" could master! As a fifth grader, his "writing" consisted of shaky scrawl that looked much like that of a first grader. It humiliated and discouraged him.

Music was the only class where David was allowed to be with the "normal" children outside the confines of the self-contained special ed room. He loved it! Blessed with a sweet, clear voice and able to carry tunes well, David easily remembered words to many popular songs, even though he couldn't recall what three minus one was!

Gradually, his enjoyment of even this class ebbed, as the teacher's red-penciled notes on the margin of his music homework, became more frequent. The notes took on a threatening tone, which alarmed us. I carefully explained in notes returned to the music teacher that we would help in every way that we could, but that the fifth-grade assignments were beyond David's first grade writing and math skills.

The teacher would place music notes into groups arranged like math problems, with a quarter note equaling a one-fourth fraction, a half note equaling a one-half fraction, etc. After the student figured out the math equivalent of each note, he/she was to add or subtract the fractions.

I told the teacher that David didn't understand the adding and subtracting of whole numbers, much less fractions, and that the assignments were a total waste of time for the teacher, David and us. They might work well with the rest of the class, but I could see no point in frustrating either himself or our son. I suggested, tactfully I hoped, in one note, that David be given something else to do for homework.

Not surprisingly, my suggestion was ignored. There followed more of the same assignments, accompanied by additional threats from the instructor, who chose not to meet with us when we requested it…several times.

The situation concluded disastrously:

Spring semester, 1979, was well underway by February 16th. That morning I made an optometric appointment for David immediately after school. Before noon, I called to let the school receptionist know that David should not ride the bus, but wait on me to pick him up.

The receptionist pleasantly agreed that she would give him and his teacher the message, never hinting that anything unusual had already taken place that day. I had no reason to suspect anything out of the ordinary as I parked in front of Bella Vista Elementary. The only clouds of which I was aware that Friday afternoon were the harbingers of snow.

As the dismissal bell sounded, the relieved teachers, followed by lively students, raced through the exit doors and disappeared, fleeing their responsibilities for the weekend.

Everyone, that is, except David.

Normally, he would have made one of the most eager exits…but, even after the more leisurely-paced kids strolled off in various directions, he was nowhere in sight.

I waited, wondering what was keeping him inside.

After a few more minutes, his diminutive teacher materialized next to the passenger door, briskly announcing, "There something I need to discuss with you."

Here we go, again… I thought, as I told her I'd be glad to listen.

"Could you please hurry, though, since David has an appointment in a few minutes?"

"Yes, I'll be brief!"

And, brief she was!

So fleeting was her story, in fact, that she failed to relate several important, truthful, details! She climbed into the car and prefaced her narrative with the verbal notation, that, "David did not complete his written assignment in class today," which was no surprise to me. He hated the slow, painful process of committing words to paper in cursive. I knew it. So did the teacher.

As a result of his failure to complete the written assignment to the teacher's satisfaction, he was banished to the hallway. Why? Because the teacher had ordered him to sit and work on it out there, separated from classmates, the object of a kind of public discipline in full view of passing teachers and students.

What was she thinking? Execution of convicted murderers isn't done as publicly as she was punishing David for his known problem…punishment for one of the very problems that caused him to be in her class!

She kept chattering, warming to the occasion and oblivious of the passing time.

I listened, wishing that she would get to the point!

And, where was David?

"Well, when I went to see if he had finished, he had not gotten his work done. Furthermore, he had wadded up his paper!"

Her declaration was in the kind of voice used by TV media to relate details of a hideous crime…

As that voice took on a different tone, her facial expression also changed. Voice and face assumed distinct frowns.

Watching her, I thought, *I don't blame him for wadding up the paper. Writing is so difficult and no teacher has bothered to teach him to spell, either. I try to help him at home, but he needs explanations at school, also!*

Apparently, he thought that if he destroyed the paper he'd be through with the aggravation of being ten years old and still reverting to first-grade-printing. At least for one day.

In addition, whenever he wasn't pleased with a paper, he wadded it up and gave himself a chance to start over with a clean sheet. The teacher also knew that as well as I did!

Our child seemed to loathe himself for his shortcoming concerning cursive writing. And, apparently he didn't blame the real culprit, the brain damage…he simply equated inability to write with "dumbness" and blamed himself.

I couldn't help thinking, *She is supposed to understand special education kids! Why did she get mad at David for not being able to write, when she knows that is a serious problem for him? He would inscribe the Gettysburg Address on her front steps, if he were able!*

It seemed to me that he had already exercised more tolerance with the writing situation than I would have! Especially, when his most careful efforts usually ended with his erasures and teacher's red marks covering the page. Even alone in the hall, he knew that he had failed to get things written neatly enough to please the teacher…that's when he wadded the paper. He had tried very hard…he knew it would not please her, so, apparently he considered that it was better to dispose of the paper than face her displeasure!

"That," she was yelling at me, "was the final straw!

"I told David that I was going to teach him a lesson!"

That, I thought, *would be a nice change! It's about time…you, teaching him.*

Teaching him, however, was not what happened! Terribly punishing him actually took place and she had to admit it to me…reconstructing the damaging details to protect herself and her career. The young woman was plainly out of control. She was livid…thrashing her arms around with her fists clinched. I thought she was going to physically attack me!

Her idea of a lesson turned out to be corporal punishment that was allowed in New Mexico, if the event were witnessed by another adult.

So, off they marched toward the principal's office, leaving the class unattended. En route, she stated, they encountered David's nemesis, The Music Teacher, who moonlighted as the music director for a local church.

Since the principal was not in his office, "I asked the music teacher if he would be my witness for David's punishment, and he said, 'No, I won't be your witness, because I want to be the person to punish David! He stuck out his tongue in class today.'"

Wow!

We were never able to determine if the "tongue episode" actually happened. Was it intended as an insult for the teacher, was it in response to another child sticking out his/her tongue at David, or was our child just passing the time of day. At any rate, the infraction—true or untrue—apparently had sufficiently annoyed the "music man," who then found his perfect and approved chance to get even with David.

Her narrative was concluding with her statement that the music teacher "hit David with a board, striking him on the left arm because David threw his arm behind his back" for protection! When we saw the board, a one by four, eighteen inches long, and found that it had been wielded by a 250-pound, over-six-foot tall man. I knew that I, too, would have tried to defend myself!

She admitted, that, David's arm was hit, and he fussed about it, saying that it hurt a lot but, (winking at me and turning her head away from David who was climbing into the back seat) "I'm sure when he gets home for the weekend, he will forget all about it. It's alright. There's nothing wrong with it."

Where did she get her medical degree and opinion?

Stunned and disbelieving, I sat, frozen in silence. Listening. Staring wordlessly at the teacher who now had a smile returning to her face. Finding my voice, I asked, "Did anyone look at his arm?"

"Oh, yes, the school nurse did. There's nothing wrong."

There she went, again, trying to convince me as well as herself, that nothing is wrong.

David, in the seat behind me and barely breathing, didn't move a muscle. He focused on some faraway, probably more pleasant circumstance...and cautiously waited.

I gripped the steering wheel, thinking, *If I occupy my hands, maybe I won't choke her!*

My initial reaction had been to hit her. Hard! Better yet, let the Music Man hit her with the board! Then she could hit him with it! How about that? Thoughts ran over each other: *What if I had not come to school today after David? What if he had not had that appointment? Would he have volunteered to tell his dad and me the story I was hearing?*

The answer was a certainty before my question was fully formed: No, he would not have told us...for two reasons: One, he seldom ratted on anyone, no matter how dreadfully he had been treated. And, two, with a gentle, pacific manner, he would at the very most, have told us he had "hurt my arm at school today," omitting details of how the injury had occurred.

I had the impression that those two teachers knew of those characteristics and counted on David's own lack of vengefulness to protect them.

Had he ridden home on the bus, he might never have even mentioned the incident...obviously, the teachers and staff were not going to bring it, voluntarily, to our attention. Except that circumstances had forced the teacher's hand and she had to tell me her version of the story.

I turned to David, as the teacher hurried back into the school building. "Son, let me see your arm."

As he pulled back his coat sleeve, what was revealed was a large, very swollen, bruised and already discolored area between his wrist and elbow, darkening and looking painful.

"Does it hurt?"

Tears filled his eyes, undermining the bravery he was attempting. "Yes, Mom, it hurts a lot. It wouldn't quit and I asked the school nurse for something to make it quit and she said I didn't need anything. She said I was just wanting attention and that my arm was alright." Sadly, he lowered his head, recalling the day's startling events.

I suspected the true nature of his injury and drove to our hospital.

"You want me to do *what?*"

My amazed husband, his attention divided between my request for an x-ray of David's arm and a patient in the exam room, hadn't quite absorbed what I was telling him.

"I want us to make an x-ray of David's arm! Right now!"

As George placed the wet film on the lighted viewbox, our suspicions were confirmed.

David's arm, indeed, was broken, the fracture running the width of the radius!

Thankfully, the fractured ends of bone were still aligned.

The next stop, at the office of the only orthopedic surgeon in Clovis, was a mistake—at least in the choice of that particular physician. It didn't occur to us until after he had looked at David and the x-rays, that this man was, also, the physician for the Clovis School System sports groups! By the time that realization soaked in, the doctor had already been told how and where the fracture occurred. Oops!

He rationalized, in some odd way, that David did not need a cast in spite of the broken bone. I wondered if he happened to be losing touch with reality. He stubbornly refused to put a cast on the arm (even after George requested it more than once)…insisting, instead, that the broken limb "only needed to be put in a sling." He was, obviously, protecting Clovis Schools, *et al.*

We felt that there was little we could do, except go along with him, even though we did not agree. We knew that David's arm needed better support as it healed, especially since this was the second time his left arm had been broken.

However, for six weeks, we conducted an ongoing battle to keep his arm in the sling. David understood, intellectually, that he needed to immobilize the arm, but, it hurt! To relieve the pain, he'd frequently remove the sling so that he could change positions with his arm…often disposing of the sling altogether. Miraculously, healing eventually took place, but not without a toll on each of us.

The attitude of the physician was only one of the obstacles we faced.

When George called the District Attorney that Friday evening, he also placed calls to our own attorneys and the Clovis Police Department, and found that each, in his own way, seemed opposed to helping us.

We had no idea why.

The DA later called the Clovis police to investigate and they cooperated by sending a female detective to our home that evening. She looked at David's arm and at the long, red and blue bruise across his upper right thigh. Then, she talked to him alone in his room, and to us, returning the following day to take individual statements from each of us, cautioning us not to talk to anyone else about what had happened.

She said that she planned, the following Monday, to go to the school and confront the two teachers involved in the incident. After she had spent several hours alone with David, she let us read his statement.

It was then, when we read his version, that we discovered:

1. The injury had occurred before noon, not just prior to my arrival at the school at 3:00 p.m.

2. David had, truthfully, been in a great deal of pain.

3. His pain and injury had been virtually ignored by his teacher and the school nurse.

4. Punishment continued after his arm was broken!

5. We were never notified nor asked to come to the school to see about him, during the entire school day. He wondered why we didn't come to school to get him!

In his statement, David mentioned that he told his teacher, after his arm was broken, that he did not feel like eating lunch. He was forced to eat, anyway. However, he was not allowed to sit in the lunchroom with the rest of the students.

Instead, he was isolated behind a portable screen, facing a blank cement wall, near the hot range in the cafeteria kitchen!

Alone, and hurting, physically and emotionally.

Amazed by the revelation about his being isolated, I asked him about it, in the presence of the detective. His only response was that he was told that he was being punished but he was never told a reason.

With the detective still listening, I asked Dave if he had ever been forced to eat in isolation in the kitchen before yesterday.

"Yes."

His quiet reply astounded and appalled us. "Yes, several times."

The look of dismay on the face of the detective must have mirrored mine, and George looked as shocked as I felt. Too, the young detective had children in the Clovis School System and she must have been thinking, *What about my children?* After all, perhaps such treatment was not unique.

Questioned further, David indicated that once in awhile another boy would be placed behind such a screen, and isolated during lunch, as some sort of punishment.

When we questioned the school officials about it, we got no answers! "Isolation" was, simply, "cruelly used." That was that!

The night after his arm was broken, we took David and John to a movie. Just as the lights dimmed, a couple paused in the aisle next to us. The tall, heavy man spoke to David, who was seated on my right. Promptly, David became wide-eyed and appeared to be frightened.

Puzzled by David's reaction, I watched him slide down in the seat, obviously trying to shrink from the gigantic man who was staring at him.

"How are you, David? How's your arm?" the man repeated, several times.

How did he—how did anyone—know about his arm?

Fright seemed to paralyze David and he couldn't answer.

The stranger persisted, "You are going to be alright, aren't you?"

Who on earth is that man and why does he keep asking about David's arm? No one knows about it. I mulled the thoughts...and then made a huge mistake by telling him, "David's arm is broken!"

As if answering me, the large couple took seats directly in front of us. The man turned around, a surprised expression on his face...then he shrugged his shoulders, mumbling, "Well, that just happens...sometimes...too bad..."

As I looked at David, he whispered, "That's the music teacher!"

The inquisitive man was the person who had broken David's arm!

Thanks a lot, Carolyn! The news was out now!

Forget the surprise visit to the school on Monday by the detective.

I turned to George, who was clenching his fists, as an ominous frown line formed between his eyebrows.

I whispered, "I'll bet that when the movie starts, he heads for the phone!" George agreed.

Sure enough, as the film started, the teacher stood, then waddled toward the back of the theater. George followed, closely enough to overhear a portion of the man's phone conversation: "The Kendalls are here, now."

My husband thought that the teacher was talking to the special education teacher, and, no matter who was on the other end of his conversation, it was certain that the special ed teacher would know soon enough about their fracturing of David's arm.

With the element of surprise ruined, by Monday morning those two instructors would have their stories in tandem, when the detective made her surprise visit to school.

And, they did!

CHAPTER TWENTY
One Lie, Then Many…

Monday dawned calm and clear, a beautiful day in eastern New Mexico. The slight breeze, stirring thin clouds around, mocked the storm currents boiling inside of George and me.

We had decided to take David out of Bella Vista, although only goodness knew where we would be able to find a classroom locally. After all, we'd been told that it was "Bella Vista or nothing" at the beginning of the school year, which now seemed much longer than only five months ago.

Busy at the clinic, George couldn't go to the school with me to collect David's records. I had started out the door to go to the school when the phone rang. The Bella Vista principal was calling to say, "I hear that there is a problem about David."

A problem about David?

"Yes, and a problem about two teachers," he admitted, saying that, "the police detective just left."

So…that's what prompted him to call! Not any concern about David or the condition of his arm or his feelings. His only concern was that "the police detective just left!"

"Yes, sir, you do have problems. I believe that you should know that I am now leaving, headed for your school, and I will be there in about ten minutes to pick up David's records."

"Why?"

I thought, "Why, indeed! So your teachers won't have another chance to abuse him." I thought better of saying that, instead explaining, "His father and I feel that he should no longer be in one of your classrooms, or in the building, or in contact with either of those two teachers who are involved in this. Just please have the records ready and I will get them."

"Well, Mrs. Kendall, I'm very sorry, but we don't have any way that we can give you the records. They are the property of the school system."

"I don't have to have the originals, copies will be sufficient."

"Well, we have another problem. You see, the only copying machine is in the office of the school administration, and it is across town." (As if I didn't know where the administration office was located.) "Perhaps by this afternoon my secretary will have time to take them there and copy them."

Gathering momentum, I hastily made my position very clear: "I will be glad to drive your secretary across town and wait while she copies the records. Right now. Goodbye."

It seemed more sensible to stop the conversation, which was, I knew, a stall on the part of the principal. I headed for the battleground.

In no more than five minutes, I parked in front of the school. As I walked into the lobby, the receptionist met me, announcing, "The principal wants to talk to you."

I wasn't surprised, as the red-faced administrator approached me, to hear him saying apologetically, "You know, we found that we do have a copying machine, and the records are being readied now."

"Where?"

"In the area behind my office."

"Thank you. I'll go watch."

"That's not necessary, Mrs. Kendall. You can wait in my office."

"Wanna bet?"

I stalked away, leaving him muttering to himself.

Bitter, salty tears formed rivulets down my makeup, mingling with mascara smudges.

I couldn't have cared less what I looked like or what he, or anyone else, thought at that moment!

I grabbed a few sheets of papers as the copier spit them out, attempting to read the reports through my blurry haze. I still wasn't sure that I was doing the right thing...I didn't have any idea what the right thing was, but at least I was doing something!

I stood in a book-lined storage area, surrounded by the trappings of elementary school life...still shocked by the events of the last several days. The emotional hurt wouldn't stop...for David or for us.

The copier, fed by the secretary and a special education diagnostician, whirred efficiently, obediently supplying the copies I wanted.

I just had no idea there was so much material in his school files. Two overloaded manila folders were crammed not only with records but I discovered they contained a great deal of unnecessary information.

I wanted copies of everything and that wasn't going to be easy, given that the papers were being sorted into "copy" and "do not copy" stacks.

"Let's have it all, please."

"Well, there is really no need for you to have anything except his academic records," the secretary stated.

"Then, why is all of this other stuff even in his files? If it is not necessary, it should not be in there."

The two women exchanged glances and grudgingly began to copy all of the material.

As Thala Stalls, diagnostician, calmly put papers into the machine, I wondered just how the school had obtained the copier so rapidly. Not ten minutes earlier the principal had insisted that he did not have one in the building and the only one available was across town.

Lo and behold, here was one...working quite well, too!

Just gobbling up reports, grade slips, nasty comments by former teachers, various evaluations. It appeared from the sheer volume that the school system must own stock in a paper mill.

The obliging copier kept on, and on, sending forth perfect renditions of David's school record.

Fast.

Nervously, Mrs. Stalls, who was a stranger to me, and the secretary, tried to make small talk.

Strained smiles passed between them, materializing and then fading. Terse sentences tentatively punctuated the uneasy quiet.

I was amazed by the revelation unfolding in my hands. I stacked my copies into neat piles, which soon covered the shrinking counter space. Occasionally, some especially interesting bits of information would be handed to me, and I accepted each of them without comment.

George and I had noticed that teachers often seemed to have a pre-conceived, built-in resentment for David. I was now discovering the reason: Their feelings could be accounted for, in large part, by the contents of the academic files.

Some of his former instructors had purposely left their hand-written, hateful notes hidden between official papers, in a trail of discontent and foreboding about our child.

We hadn't seen any of this disgusting material because, until quite recently, parents had not been permitted access to their children's school records. Also, there was no reason for us to even guess that such papers existed.

This is a bad dream...no, a nightmare! Soon, I'll wake up...I'll find that his arm wasn't broken...these files aren't real...and I'm not seeing all of this...

Wishful thinking.

It was hard to believe some of the remarks, comments by disgruntled instructors who were unable to meet the challenge of educating David. It appeared that they sought to vindicate themselves by taking out on David their anger for their own inadequacies. They must have hoped that future teachers would agree that David was incorrigible...unteachable...a Disaster Waiting to Happen.

Many of the items in the files were stamped across the front, in large black letters: **NOT TO BE SEEN BY PARENTS!**

It was no wonder they were being kept under wraps and away from us.

George and I found these stamped items among the most interesting! They contained some of the most objectionable comments about David, his problems and his capabilities, plus sidelight comments about us, his parents!

What an eye-opening experience: We finally saw, in writing, comments that were directly opposed to what the writers had been telling us in person!

Which had been their true thoughts and which were lies?

Why was this disgusting, secretive method used to communicate information to future teachers and undermine any confidence they might have developed about David?

More to the point, what was to be gained by collecting and disseminating this written garbage?

We had no answers.

Only the people who wrote the comments could answer those questions.

An hour passed, then thirty more minutes.

I wished it were all finished. Certainly I was unwelcome and I felt terribly alone. Even lonelier as I continued to see what had actually been passed along from one school and one teacher to another for six years.

And, then, those darned tears!

I wondered why I couldn't be composed...collect myself and stop the droplets. Discouragement wrapped itself around me: Years of trying so hard to help...and now this!

The final blow came as the signed punishment slip was placed into my hands.

It was a requirement in New Mexico that when corporal punishment was administered, a form was to be completed both by the person requesting the punishment as well as by the person who administered it. The official version in this case included a signed slip complete with an underlined notation that only one blow was administered.

The fact that the comment was in different color ink and on the back of the slip made it appear that it had been added after the slip was originally filled out. And, it did seem strange to me that it was underlined.

The other fact was that although these people wanted us—as well as the police—to believe that David had only been hit once with the wooden paddle, he had a fracture of the left arm between elbow and wrist, and an injured right thigh. We didn't understand how both injuries could have occurred with only *one* blow.

Of course, anatomically, it wasn't possible.

The copying was finally completed. Breaking the heavy silence, I half-whispered to Mrs. Stalls, who seemed saddened about the situation and wanting to help, "We'd give anything...everything...just to know what happened to David to have caused his brain damage. We've never been able to find out and doctors just seem to keep blaming me...we need to know *what* his problem is and *how* to help him."

Not really expecting an answer, I started picking up the papers and was ready to leave.

Mrs. Stalls looked up, in disbelief. "You mean, that, no one ever told you?"

I nodded.

"That's right. We've spent time, money...effort. You know how much testing David's been subjected to and all for nothing. No answers.

"And, look at the mess we're in, now. We can't leave him in that classroom, or even in this school building. What if the next punishment is worse than this?"

More tears...but this time they came from Mrs. Stalls.

Glancing at the floor in embarrassment, then at Mrs. Stalls and me, the secretary seemed interested to hear the diagnostician's response.

Someone interested? How earth-shaking!

"Have you heard of Dr. George Brown in Albuquerque? He's a wonderful pediatrician and works with all sorts of handicapped children. He writes books on special kids, travels around the world teaching others how to help them. Maybe he can give you some answers.

"I'll get his address for you right now…and his phone number."

Dazed, I watched her hurry down the hall, returning nearly instantly, clutching the sheet of paper that was a renewal of hope for us.

Lord! Just like that!

Entering the building in frustration, emerging with expectancy!

I bubbled over with questions, grabbed the remaining papers and scrambled out the door.

Hope was still alive!

CHAPTER TWENTY-ONE
Finally, Another Answer!

"Yes, Dr. Brown is in his office. He'll be happy to talk to you."

The warmth of the receptionist's greeting spanned the 250 miles separating us, giving me hope for the first time in many discouraging months.

Pleasantly surprised, I noticed that Dr. Brown didn't sound like many of the others who had seen, and dismissed, David.

"Certainly, I'd be glad to see David, as soon as it's convenient for you."

Convenient for us?

After almost ten years of searching?

We'd have headed for Albuquerque that instant if necessary!

"Of course, send me all of the information that you can round up, from birth until now, test results, evaluations, anything…everything. I'll look it over before I examine your son. Now, we'll set up your appointment for three weeks from today. And, I'd like to talk to you and Dr. Kendall before I see David."

Another surprise: We didn't have to scramble through the usual interference run by a doctor's receptionist. It amazed me to hear that Dr. Brown made his own appointments.

Three days later I watched my parcel holding David's history as it started toward Albuquerque. I'd tried to include everything that might be helpful to the physician, plus our own personal observations.

Excitement was contagious and our home took on a lighter tone and a more encouraging outlook.

"Maybe it was almost worth the assault on David, his broken arm and everything else. At least we found out about all of the junk in his school file and then we were pointed to Dr. Brown…and he has the expertise to help us."

We kept David out of school for a week, and then approached the superintendent's office in search of a classroom for him.

Imagine our shock when one was located! Immediately! And, of all things, after we were told at the start of the fall term, that, there was no other place for him except the ghetto school. Now, in February, there was a place nearby, in another elementary school in our district, away from unpleasant memories. It had been there all of the time with special ed classes.

The move was not without a price, though. In order for David to be placed at Barry Elementary, we had to sign papers acknowledging his "B.D." (Behavior Disordered) condition!

We weighed that bit of news against the alternative: Find a full-time tutor or an institutionalized setting of some sort. Black or white…no gray areas. Another ultimatum: "Behavior Disordered"…or nothing!

My husband and I shared the opinion that the B.D. classification would have been more appropriately applied to some of David's teachers and school administrators! Somehow it didn't seem fair that our child should suffer the broken arm, peer humiliation, and successive undesirable classroom situations. Now, he was also to be burdened with an oppressive emotional name tag. Add that to his voluminous school files?

Given no other choices, we signed the papers allowing David to complete the school year in a classroom.

The B.D. classroom, in spite of its designation, was for the most part orderly and relatively quiet. An all-male group of about a half dozen students comprised the class. Their various levels of abilities and achievements, along with divergent emotional problems, kept their instructor, Susan Hare, moving at a gallop.

There was a blessing in the limited enrollment. Most of the time there were few youngsters in the class, and with the assistance of an extremely capable aide, Susan actually taught kids who were labeled unteachable.

Unlovable might have been added to the children's character assessments.

From broken homes and some near-poverty levels, the boys provided a challenge. David was, usually, one of the only students from a two-parent family, and he was more fortunate than most others by having parental support.

There were the usual hazards to be overcome, as David settled into the routine of his new class, but he found that school could be a good place to spend a day!

Frequently, Susan's patience with all of her charges was pushed to the extreme…and beyond…but she worked through the shell with which David had surrounded himself.

He became responsive, then eager.

A light at the end of the tunnel? Or just the train coming toward us?

After a couple of weeks in the class, I received an urgent call at 8:30 one morning, with Susan in tears and asking me to come after David. For some reason he had become close to violent…and was shouting and hollering threats at her, the principal and other children. He was totally out of control. The burden of the past several weeks had become more than he could manage, and he was resisting in the only manner that he knew, taking out on teachers the feelings he thought they had taken out on him!

Agitated and unreachable, he marched to the car, climbed in and slammed the door.

"Well, son, what's wrong? Don't you know you frightened her…and the other children? What's wrong?"

He crossed his arms, stared out of the window and sullenly refused to answer.

I drove home, sadly wondering if we'd placed too much hope in this new class…and wishing that the next week would pass in a hurry so that we could see Dr. Brown.

Later in the morning, I called Dr. Bill Lowe, a clinical psychologist in Clovis, who agreed to visit with David that afternoon. Dr. Lowe, following an hour with him, agreed that life had simply become unbearable for David and he had more problems than he could manage. We spent only the one session with Dr. Lowe, feeling that Dr. Brown might offer alternative solutions when we saw him.

At worst, even if he couldn't offer help, *per se*, it was possible that he would be able to tell us how David's problems started.

Our encouragement was reinforced when we had our first glimpse of Dr. Brown, an imposing man who instilled confidence just by his presence.

He delightfully fulfilled our expectations, looking the way we imagined he would. Soft-spoken and a careful listener, Dr. Brown spent two hours with George and me while his nurse entertained David. The doctor didn't want to examine or even talk with David until he had an in-depth view of his background.

We were in for more pleasant surprises. Dr. Brown had actually read everything we'd sent to him! What a novel idea! We considered it to be just short of miraculous, especially since he had a large practice with unceasing demands on his time.

Obviously, he'd not only read, but digested, the information he'd received. There was none of the repetitive questioning we'd undergone so many other, tiring times. Now, we listened to fresh, previously unasked, questions.

This was followed by his observant, two-hour, unhurried examination of David while we waited outside. Then, there was another two-hour conference with the doctor, scheduled the following morning.

In the waiting room, shivers of anticipation reminded me that, after *ten years*, in another *ten minutes* we might have some answers.

What an answer we heard!

"First of all," skipping preliminaries Dr. Brown launched into his discussion, "if anyone ever told you, Carolyn, that you were the cause of David's problems—any of them—then that was just so much ---- ----!"

He efficiently filled in the blanks!

I felt that my heart was going to race through the top of my head! "I knew it! I knew it!" I heard myself repeating. "Yes, I've been told that lots of times, and I knew it wasn't true."

"You didn't cause anything. You are, all three of you, the innocent victims of a circumstance over which no one had any control. I am sure of that."

Measured baritone syllables, imparting information we'd longed to hear: "As you know, David's not retarded. He has normal intelligence."

"We know that!"

"You were accurate in assessing his problems, and I feel you've done everything that you could, to help him, given the lack of assistance and encouragement from all of the professionals who've seen him."

Next, the one question we most desired to have answered: "Do you know what caused his problems?"

"Yes, I feel certain that I do. You know, I've spent years working with handicapped children with all kinds of problems and my experience leads me to believe that either before his birth, or during the birth process, David *suffered a cerebral hemorrhage!*"

Bombshell!

Immediately, my thoughts returned to the single sheet, two-paragraph report we'd received from the adoption agency shortly before David's second birthday. We'd asked the agency for any information that might be helpful for David and us. We were told, "...arteriosclerosis, both grandmothers; grandfather's death due to cerebral hemorrhage..."

For some unknown reason, that information wasn't included in the background material I had given to Dr. Brown and without benefit of that knowledge, he had still correctly diagnosed David. The genetic tendency had become reality in the fetal stage of David's life. No one else had considered the information about the grandparents to be significant and I'd overlooked and forgotten about it.

Dr. Brown based his diagnosis on his findings with David, which included a thorough physical exam, showing the slight differences that occur in the body of a young, growing victim who has suffered cerebral hemorrhage.

What about his future, now that the origin of his problem had been defined.

A lot of territory was covered in the next two hours, and was recapped in a three-page letter forty-eight hours later:

...background...extensive speech therapy, psychological testing, problems with symbolic material, especially written language...very uncertain in number skills, transient retention of number facts, inability to visualize the symbolic image that is required for thinking about numbers, especially abstract numbers...

...interest in music and singing...in activities that involve direct manipulation or physical contact with the task...

...does not do well with abstract concepts...with theoretical or complex word tasks...

...Unusually distractible...somewhat restless and giddy (during examination)...difficulty with rapid repetitive movement and with organizing rhythmic movement. I had the impression that his left hand and left leg might be slightly different size that his right side...

...somewhat uncertain in discussing topics like money, common materials and common verbal abstractions...

...he looks about one year older than his actual age, which is deceptive to some adults who might set expectations higher than appropriate in some situations...

...(with parents) we reviewed the relationship between behavior control and word processing skills...

David has had difficulty with temperament, attention, restlessness, and uneven controls of behavior since early infancy. These difficulties with attention and impulse control are due to neurological impairment, not to psychological or social factors.

He is not suffering from a psychological or mental problem, he is having difficulties because of a neurological impairment, probably dating from birth.

He had difficulty with control of mood, attention and concentration. He tends to overreact in some situations, just as he tends to persist in some thoughts and activities. He is sometimes unpredictable, with variable moods and variable performance from one time or situation to another.

These variations in mood and skills are, also, neurological, not emotional. He has some difficulty expressing himself in words, because of his articulation problems and because of his uneven word retrieval skills.

He has difficulty imaging symbolic material, especially numbers and words, and this accounts for his extreme frustration with number tasks and his great difficulty in attempting to write out words, even on subjects that are known to him.

Clearly, Dr. Brown understood the multiplicity of the manifestations of David's prenatal mishap. Not only did he understand, he cared.

The doctor and we discussed numerous approaches to the problems, and then the information was shared with the school system.

Academically, we were hopeful and making plans. Emotionally, trying to resolve the broken arm situation, we walked into a blank wall.

CHAPTER TWENTY-TWO
Justice—Just Out of Reach

"Whatever happened to *justice?* How did it quietly slip into oblivion, to be replaced by mockery? Why is it alright for a teacher to break a child's arm at school, then go unpunished?"

I was finding it difficult to absorb the meaning of the words, as I read the letter from the Curry County District Attorney. It said, in essence, that the investigation into the situation involving David at Bella Vista School had been completed...and, that his office and the police department were "satisfied that there was no wrong-doing."

I wondered if, in that case, they thought there was some right-doing about it!

"How can this be?" George and I asked each other. "That teacher is going to be allowed to keep on teaching, with not so much as a reprimand. If David had taken that paddle and had broken the arm of that teacher, or another child, you can bet that somebody, somewhere, would have called him and us to answer for it," we agreed.

A couple of weeks had passed since his arm was broken and Dr. Brown had made his diagnosis. We were doing our best to settle back into our lives but occasionally something would jump up and take a whack at us in the most hurtful way.

Unexpectedly, many of the stabs came from people who were our "friends." One memorable night at the close of a sorority meeting, several weeks following the arm incident, the other members and I were visiting and enjoying refreshments. I walked into the kitchen of my friend's home, set my plate and cup down and started to leave. Another member blocked my path, stating, "Oh, I heard about David at school. You know what my boss told me that his wife said? You know, she's a teacher and she said that David got what he deserved!"

Her boss, by the way, was a professional man enjoying a very large practice in the community.

Stunned, I stood and looked at her. No one else had heard her comment, thank goodness, for the embarrassment that swept over me was humiliating and I felt like striking out at her...or her boss...or his wife...someone.

I didn't say anything, which was unusual, because I'm seldom at a loss for words. I picked up my coat, again headed for the door and felt the sting of tears once more sliding down my face.

The hostess, my best friend, approached, touching my arm and softly asking, "What's wrong?" All I could manage was a shrug of my shoulders as I closed the door.

The physical pain of the encounter cut right through me...and I wondered, *Is it possible that many people in this town are condemning our son for the violent act of someone else?*

It took several minutes of waiting in my car before I dared walk into our home and face George. He'd know immediately that something was wrong...and I knew that he had reached the saturation point, as we all had, trying to cope with all of the problems including those that other people shoved in our faces.

When he heard what had been said, his first reaction was to face the man whose comments had been related to me. That, of course, would not accomplish anything except to add fuel to whatever fire was already smoldering.

Probably better to forgive, even though *forgetting* was a different matter, both the comments and the district attorney's letter.

We didn't believe that we felt vindictive, but we did believe that some kind of justice should be resolved for David.

We discussed the case with several local attorneys, each of whom refused to do anything to help us. The last resort was a referral at Albuquerque where we spent several hundred dollars with two attorneys, each of whom assured us that going to court would be pointless.

The only reasons we would have sued the teacher and the school system would have been for medical expenses we had encountered and financial recovery to help with David's educational expenses. We had nothing else in mind.

Except, that we did not feel the classroom was the appropriate place for the man who had injured David (and who also was the choir director for a children's group at one of the local churches!)

After visiting with the lawyers, we found that the State of New Mexico had a law which protected public employees, including teachers, from prosecution for acts committed on the job!

Well! It certainly worked in this case! And, to think that if we had broken the leg of any dog or cat entrusted to our veterinary care, we would have been held responsible and no doubt we would have been sued and our insurance company would have been required to pay damages. Yet, those two teachers were allowed to merrily go on their way. Something really wrong with that picture!

Additionally, the attorneys assured us that while anyone can sue anyone else for anything, actually getting the case to trial as well as getting a favorable judgment and finally collecting any compensation awarded would be time consuming, financially draining and subject David to perhaps years of rehashing the experience.

We were told that David would be subjected to witness stand experiences for which he lacked the maturity. The entire series of events that could occur might, in all likelihood, be years in litigation, resulting in unnecessary trauma for him and us.

The biggest loser could be David, if he were constantly reminded about what had happened. His guilt already plainly, painfully, showed in his relationships with family and peers.

Revenge would not have been a good motive, had we filed a lawsuit. We felt that we could not let ourselves become victims of hateful feelings and we decided that our son had already been plagued enough by negative experiences.

The only option was to forget about suing the system and the teachers. We just counted the hours, miles and financial cost of the consultations with attorneys as experience.

When a little time passed and we had done nothing in court against the school system, relief must have been high among administrators and teachers. We noticed that clients of ours, who were also part of the school system and who had quit bringing in their pets for George's medical care, once more slowly began returning with their pets for treatment.

Even my cousin, who was a local elementary teacher, had not spoken to us for months. Gradually, he found time to once again visit with us.

Sometimes, situations were resolved in ways that we could not have anticipated.

David's special education teacher who had wanted David punished the day his arm was broken left Clovis at the end of the school term after she and her husband divorced.

The superintendent and his nurse-wife (who had forced us to have the unneeded testing at Amarillo) announced their retirement in order to become missionaries in a foreign country. Not, however, before he finally half-heartedly and very belatedly apologized for what had happened to David. The idea for the apology did not originate with him, either…and he made certain that was understood by us.

Although we were not going to court, George and I felt that we should make some sort of official report. We thought it might help to prevent the same dreadful circumstances from happening to another defenseless child. After all, perhaps the next child who was hit with the board might be smaller and even more helpless than David had been…

Finding a person or group to whom we could talk about the problem was not easy, but finally the opportunity arrived. Seven members of the Special Education Evaluation and Credentials Committee from the New Mexico Board of Education came to Clovis.

We accidentally found out about the impending visit when we saw a small article buried in the middle section of *The Clovis News Journal*. This was followed by a call to us from the mother of another special ed child. She told us that the committee members would meet with a select parent-teacher group during the four-day visit.

She heartily laughed, stating that the meeting was planned so that parents of special education youngsters could give a pat on the back to the local program!

Only parents who were informed about the various phases of the program and who were known to be in agreement with the system had been invited. Neither she, nor we, had been asked to attend…not surprising to us.

However, as it was a public meeting about a section of the public school, we felt that we had a right to go. We began gathering our courage...our information...and our complaints so that we could enter the lions' den.

Amused, we watched the shocked expressions on the faces of administrators and staff members as we were seated and the meeting began.

We sat quietly through the two-hour meeting. At the conclusion, tension was high when the chairman asked for comments from the parents. Several glances were shot in our direction. We made no public response and as the meeting adjourned, we handed each member of the committee a three-page letter.

Then we left.

Our document briefly outlined some of the many problems we had experienced with the local school system, not limiting our observations to David's broken arm, but including other items such as the two encounters with the superintendent's wife at our home.

We also stated that we believed the local educational situation was failing to educate our son and that the tragic occurrence was a result of the failure of the system. We believed, and said as much, that breaking a child's arm seemed to be harsh punishment, especially since his crime was one of not being able to write! And that was one of the reasons he was even in the special ed program!

Adding insult to injury was the fact that his writing arm was the one that had been broken.

Had there been any logic in the situation of breaking the arm of a child who cannot write in order to discipline him for not writing, such logic escaped us!

After we returned home, we wondered to each other if we would actually hear from anyone.

The waiting period was very brief: The night following the credentials meeting, the evaluators and school administrators met and shared their investigative findings...sharing, also, the contents of our letter!

By 8:00 a.m. the next morning, the superintendent was calling our home, mysteriously full of pseudo-apologies.

He was, "sorry that David's arm was broken...that you have borne the entire medical expenses...that you've had no official apology."

He "regretted" what he called his "lack of sensitivity for not calling sooner and offering assistance..."

For several minutes he rattled on with profuse conciliatory expressions, while I quietly listened.

When he finally paused long enough for me to at least get into the conversation, I assured him that we had "managed to cope" thus far.

"Is there anything that I...we...can do? Can we help you with expenses? Is there anything?"

"As a matter of fact, there is one thing..."

"What?"

I smothered a laugh as I dismissed the idea of asking for either a million dollars or for him to jump off the roof, and, instead, requested that David's school files be purged of the nasty, uncalled-for-comments by teachers.

"Of course, of course. We'll get together right away with the director of Special Education, David's principal, his teacher and you and Dr. Kendall. When do you want to meet?"

His obliging attitude was somewhat disconcerting, but I grabbed the calendar and suggested a time the next week, which he accepted. If this were all we were going to ask, he certainly was going to try to appease us!

The "academic file review committee" (everything has a title) met, early one May morning, opening files and examining every scrap of paper, one sheet at a time.

All prejudicial documents were purged.

We found that our definition of the word purge wasn't quite the same as that of the school officials, but at least the more abusive inflammatory statements were sealed where current and future teachers no longer had access to them.

Of course, we would rather have seen them destroyed, but that wasn't done.

Closing the session, we felt that perhaps now David had a file that was approaching what it should have been all along: an accumulation of his scholastic scores and achievements, rather than a dumping ground for written material gathered from disgruntled, spiteful teachers.

Some small amount of justice, meager as it was, had actually been accomplished!

CHAPTER TWENTY-THREE
Language Matters...

"Love," otherwise named Susan Hare and Carolyn Luck, became part of David's life at the end of the spring semester. They began working to reshape many areas of difficulty.

After the dreadful day when David's emotional control hit zero in Susan's class, we were afraid that she might not want to work with him. To our relief, she warmly welcomed him back into her classroom and continued to work with him.

Carolyn Luck, whose title was Director of Special Education, had one of the most unenviable professional responsibilities in the school system. On her shoulders fell all of the problems and decision making, long range planning and split-second decisions that are a part of the life of every true leader.

Each of these beautiful women, so dedicated to her profession...so serious in their pursuit of excellence for their handicapped students, became willing to listen, to talk and to share!

It didn't happen, of course, in the first few weeks that Dave was in Susan's class, but by the end of the semester it was obvious that at long last he had a teacher who was implementing productive plans for him in the classroom.

He began to show improvement in his work and we were aware that he was actually *learning*, not just passing the time of day at school.

Thala Stalls, the diagnostician to whom we owed a great debt of thanks for pointing us to Dr. Brown, tenderly gave careful attention to details for David's educational progress. (She also became a much-appreciated pet owner at our hospital.)

George and I began to feel that even if we were still in the midst of the war, at least we were making progress in a battle!

Assuredly, teamwork would accomplish positive results much sooner than discord!

It took time…and lots of effort…by everyone.

No matter that David's academic situation appeared more hopeful, George and I continued to disapprove of the B.D. label placed on him. In May, we refused to sign placement papers for him to be in another B.D. classroom the next semester.

Two months passed and the matter had not been resolved.

Finally, there arrived a representative of the Health, Education and Welfare Department located in Dallas. We naively thought he was there because of our complaint. We had entered a formal complaint for failure to teach, as well as for child abuse, to the HEW office at Dallas. Time passed and we heard nothing from them. David seemed to be making progress in Susan's class and we assumed HEW was not going to so much as even answer our complaint.

At the close of a sweltering New Mexico July work day, I received a call from a gentleman who identified himself as being with the HEW office. He said that he was in Clovis to discuss the problem and wanted us to meet with him and Carolyn Luck that evening.

George had one of his frequent emergencies and couldn't go to the meeting, so I went alone, to the neutral site…a decaying block-square building that housed the original Clovis Campus, Eastern New Mexico University.

The oppressive heat smothered any attempts at congeniality. The stale air refused to circulate through the shrunken office, where there was barely room for the three of us to be seated.

The atmosphere dripped with humidity and sarcasm. Boring repetition set in early and lodged itself firmly in place; a litany of David's problems followed by school "attempts to correct."

The bureaucrat didn't appear concerned about our charge of child abuse. Neither did he mention the allegations of "failure to teach."

His overriding concern was that I should sign the placement form for the Behavior Disordered classroom...then he could get back to his air-conditioned motel room!

"Hurry!"

"Get it over with!"

"Don't be obstinate!"

Back and forth, circling the room, the bits of conversation mercilessly droned on.

"No, David cannot be placed into a classroom with any other label on it. B.D. is where we want him next year and that's where he will be placed!"

I repeatedly explained our family's position that we thought the teaching that was done in the current classroom was fine, but we did not like having David labeled "behavior disordered" when that wasn't his problem!

Patience was at a premium.

Listen...talk...around and around...the carousel in my brain began to pick up speed.

Repetition was now entrenched. I explained, again, why we didn't agree with the B.D. label, especially in view of Dr. Brown's letter. George and I were convinced that eventually such a classification would be an academic "kiss of death" for David.

Those two words, Behavior Disordered, spelled T-R-O-U-B-L-E and we knew it!

"Who wants to be encumbered with such a designation?"

"I'm sorry, but that's the name of the room."

"Who, really, wants to teach someone if he bears such a label?"

Mrs. Luck assured me, time and again, that such a classification was "for paperwork purposes, only." It was, she promised, "really meaningless."

Meaningless?

Maybe.

We weren't talking about her children!

"Then, if you believe that's the room where he needs to be, go ahead and place him there. Just call it something else on his records!"

The topic had been discussed so frequently at home that I was sure of George's opinion, and we agreed that B.D. was discriminatory. It was a mark against our child, who already had a lifetime accumulation of marks against him!

As far as we were concerned, it screamed inadequacies, it forecast failure and it reinforced doubt about David.

Monotonously, the minutes wearily ticked past. Nine p.m. and sunset approached, illuminating the gloomy gray walls with a somewhat cheerier glow. The stifling heat remained.

Losing interest in the conversation, I began to concentrate on the variety of patterns left by long-departed paint flakes.

The single, bare, bulb, dangling from the ceiling on its threadbare wire, offered only the most meager light in the arriving darkness. The summer night settled heavily around us.

My calm exterior was dissolving, as The Texan presented one aspect, then another…different view of the same solution: Sign the placement paper!

"If I'd known what we'd be discussing, I would have stayed at home," I admonished myself.

Suddenly, my merry-go-round screeched to a halt!

"Would you repeat that, Mrs. Luck? I'm not sure that I understood."

Carolyn looked at me, and I heard her saying what I had been suggesting the entire evening. "If another classification were applied to David, would that let you then sign his placement papers?"

Amazed, I nodded agreement.

"Certainly, depending on what it is. That's all we wanted."

Hurriedly, Mrs. Luck re-worded the form, and then handed it to me after we agreed on the wording, which would be less accusing and defamatory.

Gratefully, I signed it.

I reminded myself silently that nothing during the preceding two hours had been said about the complaint that George and I had made to HEW. For his part, the government representative probably hoped that I had forgotten about it altogether.

I, of course, had not! It just seemed easier, accepting his role as mediator for the title of the placement form, rather than having him try to settle anything else.

I felt sure that David's best interest would be served by closing the matter as gracefully as possible.

Nothing more could be accomplished now, by my stubbornly clinging to martyrdom in his behalf.

During the evening it had become obvious that Carolyn Luck had joined George, Susan and me in our conviction that David was worthwhile…worth teaching…worth salvaging…worth all the effort that it would take to start all over again, practically at first-grade level, to build a whole person.

We began!

CHAPTER TWENTY-FOUR
Birthday Party, Anyone?

"Beginning again" contained at least one surprise element. Susan Hare changed classrooms and, once again, David would have a different teacher. We thought it would be just one more in the passing parade.

The new school year dawned, however, with a very special teacher for special education. Jim Nesbitt had recently graduated from college and brought to his all-male class an energetic attitude that made him seem more-than-able to cope with the problem-plagued boys.

Once more, most of the children seemed to be from one-parent homes with unstable lifestyles in the most minimal surroundings. There appeared to be very little positive reinforcement in their lives. A few shared homes with their grandparents who frequently understood neither the necessity of, nor the purpose for, the placement of their grandchildren in special education classes.

Sizes and ages in the class varied as much as their ethnic backgrounds. These students were victims of circumstances that they were too young to understand. They were forced into a kind of comradeship by their mutual disabilities.

Jim immediately established himself as a stern disciplinarian, who loved and tried to understand his students. In return, the boys eventually responded to his concern and David's attitude became more positive as the semester progressed.

For four semesters, David diligently strived in Jim's non-graded classroom. Sometimes, situations were shaky, but teacher and students maintained mutual respect. More than that, the pupils began to learn how wonderful it is to both receive and to give care.

Learning took place every day. Not always in leaps and bounds, but, at least, steadily.

David began to see that he could do better…and an unaccustomed feeling of pride in his schoolwork enveloped him.

One rather troublesome issue reared its ugly head, when the principal began calling frequently and I had to leave work, go to the school after David. The standard complaint was that David was fighting during recess.

After each of these events of retrieving David, George would ask him if he were actually fighting. David always replied, "Yes!"

"Why?"

"The other kids call me bad names and hit me."

When I was out of town one day, the principal made a tactical error and called George, requesting that he come after David. As he was prepped for and going into surgery, George had neither the time nor patience for this interruption…and he expressed as much to the principal.

However, George took a minute to quiz the principal about the fighting and if the other kids were hitting David and calling him names.

"Yes."

"You're always sending David home…what are you doing to the kids who are causing all the problem?"

"Nothing…there's too many of them."

At that point, I was told, George informed the principal about what would happen if we got another call to get David at school: "I'll come to the school and clean your plow!"

Re-thinking what he'd just said, and realizing that he could be in for a bit of explaining, George revised his statement, saying, "That's not a *threat*, that's a *promise!*"

Two weeks later, when we were in the school lunchroom with David, the principal came to our table and we asked him how things were going. He replied, "They couldn't be better!"

We never had any more calls requesting us to come get David...Simple solution to a silly problem. We later wondered if this action had been so effective why we hadn't used it sooner.

***

Eighteen months later, David was junior high age. He had developed determination and fine-honed his built-in endurance although it still suffered frequently from his feelings of frustration.

We saw that he was beginning to have some hope for his own future.

Then, another junction on his academic road: What would happen to him when he were placed into a much larger school, with students who were significantly more sophisticated...and where there was an alteration in the size and kind of classroom he had always been in?

No longer would he be in the sheltered atmosphere, albeit segregated, of the type in elementary school. ("Middle school" was not a concept in the school system until several years later.)

He was just now starting to have a little self-confidence and that delicate, unstable condition could so easily be shattered during the sensitive secondary years.

George and I talked about it with each other, with David and we also asked the professional advice of Carolyn Luck. She suggested that we visit a smaller school in nearby Texico, New Mexico, a very small town on the Texas-New Mexico border.

A few words with the principal and a visit to the school helped all of us to decide that this might be a better place for him during seventh grade. The entire student body numbered less than 100 and it appeared that they had fewer social problems than the larger schools in Clovis.

It can't hurt to try, we thought, *and it might be just the place for him.*

At enrollment time, he was placed with Gina Piazza's special ed students, integrating into a regular class or two after our first parent-teacher conference.

"David's much too intelligent to be in this class full-time. He needs the challenge and stimulation of other classrooms and I'm sure that some of the other teachers are willing to work with him," she explained.

So, another experimental situation was underway.

Three weeks into the semester, David's thirteenth birthday approached. As we had one child, John, with many friends, and another son, David, with almost no friends, we had made it a custom to celebrate birthdays as family-only occasions. That way, we hoped, David wouldn't notice the obvious, that John was surrounded by admiring youngsters and friends of all sorts, while he was not as fortunate.

He was the only person I ever knew who grew into a teenager without ever having a single person other than his older brother, whom he could call a friend.

At any rate, this year, his thirteenth birthday on September 4th, was to be observed in the same way with a family dinner, cake and presents. Or, so we thought.

The fly in the ointment came when his grandmother called a few weeks ahead of time, inquiring what kind of party he planned and how many people he would be inviting. George and I tried to dismiss his questioning after he talked to her, but his persistence eventually wore us down.

On Monday night before his birthday the following Saturday, his pleadings finally crushed my resistance, and I agreed that he could buy some invitations and mail them to his friends.

Jumping on his bike, he flew to the store, returning shortly with a package of party invitations. He carefully addressed, stamped and mailed eight of them to boys in his Sunday school class whom he considered to be his friends. I tried to prepare him for the inevitable: No one would show up.

I reminded him that, as always, his birthday was during the Labor Day weekend and lots of people would be out of town. Too, the invitations would not arrive at the boys' homes until Wednesday or Thursday and perhaps people would have made other plans by that time.

He put his phone number in the RSVP space...

And waited.

When no calls came on Thursday night, he called five of the boys. Each of them said that he would not be there, for a variety of reasons. He couldn't reach the other three.

Friday evening, as we put out the colorful birthday paper plates, napkins and favors, David wondered aloud about the remaining three. I finally suggested that he should call them while we waited for George to finish up at the hospital.

The first two told him, flatly, no, they would not be at his party. They would be out of town.

The last name belonged to a boy whom he considered to be his best friend although I felt the child just barely tolerated David.

I tried not to listen to the discussion, but I could see the hurt expression on David's face, and I heard his soft quizzing of the other boy, "Are you coming to my party tomorrow?"

"Why not?"

"Oh."

Then, even more softly, with a pleading quality that brought tears to my eyes, I heard him say, "Would it be alright if I went with you?"

"Oh."

Tomorrow, he would be a teenager. Tonight he was a badly bruised child, once again hurt by people whom he trusted, and he could not fight his own tears any longer.

Embarrassed by the rebuff of his "friends" and by his emotional reaction to it, he turned his back to me and hung his head, trying to regain control.

"David, honey, I wanted to spare you this…I wanted you to think, when I refused to let you plan a party, that I was just being cranky, or even mean. I'd rather have had you mad at me than to see you hurt like this," I tried to comfort him as I put my arms around my younger son.

It really was hard to think of him as not being our baby anymore, but he was already taller than I, approaching manhood and the new kinds of challenges that would bring.

He went to his room and I walked into John's room.

"Son, I have something to ask of you."

"Sure, Mom. What?"

"You know that tomorrow is your brother's birthday and he planned a party. The eight kids that he invited won't be coming," I announced, noticing the shocked expression replacing John's ever-present smile.

"Why not!"

"That's a good question, but probably because they don't like David very much, and most of them simply don't want to be around him. The worst of it is, when he called his "best friend" just now, the last one on his list, he was told that instead of coming to David's party, this other boy is going to the movies…and, it's one he's seen twice already! That's probably the poorest of the excuses David was given!

"It really makes me mad, but there's nothing I can do except try to make the day as pleasant as possible for Dave. So, would you make an extra effort to be kind to him? Maybe you and Dad and I can help him get over the pain of it."

John had always had a "rock 'em, sock 'em, get-right-to-the-point" personality, and it now erupted: "Who did this to him? How about if I talk some sense into them?"

"No, son, that won't help. We just have to make the best of what's happened. If they don't want to be here, talking won't do anything."

I left him, pondering what would be some sort of solution to the problem. The answer came the next morning, at 6:00!

Now, that was a most unusual time for John to get up when he was home on weekends from military school. (John had begged for two years to go to the premier New Mexico Military Institute at Roswell in order to get a better education than public school offered. When he was barely fourteen and ready for his freshman year, we paid the tuition and let him go. He loved it, made lifelong friends and great grades, serving as a class officer, riding with the cavalry unit and graduating with honors two weeks before he was eighteen.)

When he was home, I usually had to threaten "mayhem and murder" to jar him loose from his bed, especially on Saturdays.

George and I couldn't believe it, when we heard him hollering at David in his best "first sergeant" manner, "Up and at 'em, Dave, time's wasting and we've got places to go and things to do. Hurry up! You can't sleep all day. Get up!"

Having completed his first year as a cadet at NMMI, John knew very well how to get a young man out of bed and on his feet *early* in the morning.

He was standing in the door of David's room, casually approaching his sleepy-eyed, groggy brother with a glass of water.

"If you're not up and dressed in five minutes, you're gonna get this water…and not to drink, either!"

Grumbling, and wondering about John's amazing departure from his usual Sleepy Saturday routine, David staggered out of bed and grabbed his jeans and shirt.

From our room at the end of the hall, George called out, "What's going on? Have you lost your mind? Where are you going at this hour?"

John's smiling face appeared briefly at our door, accompanied by a wink and a promise, "Don't worry, we'll be fine. See you two in a few hours!"

We returned to bed as we heard our old clunker pickup start up and chug away down the street. At fifteen, John had a driver's license and they were on their way…to who-knew-where,

Four hours later, two laughing boys walked through the front door, David carrying a package and looking extremely pleased. John followed, all grins and just as pleased with himself.

No wonder!

John had taken David to a truck stop for breakfast, knowing that eating was David's delight in life, and let him choose anything and as much of whatever was on the menu. The list of gourmet delights ranged from sausage and potatoes and eggs to biscuits and gravy and homemade sweet rolls. It must have taken an hour just to eat all that they ordered!

The most amazing thing was, that, John had actually paid the entire bill…this was our elder son who never parted with his own money if he could "con" someone else into paying!

As if that weren't enough, they rode around until the stores opened, then John bought David presents of the Atari games he'd been wanting. At the price I knew they were, this was another surprise for us!

"Hey, guys, do you have any room left for, say, some birthday cake and ice cream?"

"Yeah, I think we can handle that!"

Shortly, we gathered around the decorated table for hamburgers and birthday cake, taking snapshots as David blew out his candles and wondering what he'd wished for. (I was afraid that I knew, but nothing could be done about his rude friends!)

One of the best pictures we have of David was made that morning, happiness shining in his eyes and the hurt gone—at least momentarily.

Once again, perhaps a bad situation had been turned into something good: When the other kids didn't want to be kind to David, it gave John a chance to spend some quality time with him and reinforce the brotherly bonds.

Things perked along at school. Miss Piazza (or "Miss Pizza" as she was known by her students) skillfully steered David through seventh grade, letting him be free to explore and learn, to participate, and to take a few more of life's knowledge knocks as well.

As unbelievable as it seemed, for the first time, a teacher actually *asked* to have David in her classroom: Joan Edwards, resource room teacher, requested that David be allowed to join her students! We appreciated the patience, kindness and caring she shared with him. A few years later, Joan and her equally wonderful husband, became clients of ours, showing equally loving care for their pet dog.

The continuing sessions that had been necessary with a speech therapist at school now became less frequent. Since David had been twenty-seven months of age someone had worked with him, building speech patterns so that he could communicate orally. He had worked hard, as had we, and the reward was clear articulation with only one or two minor problem areas.

In May, David was startled to hear his name called at the awards presentation in the school gym…not once, but *three times!*

He was used to seeing certificates and proof of achievement on John's walls, but not in his room.

However, we proudly framed and hung the certificates, which declared:

Most Improved 7th Grade Social Studies Student

Most Improved 7th Grade Career Education Student

Outstanding Reading Ability, which was accompanied by a gold medal.

What a difference caring people were making in his life!

CHAPTER TWENTY-FIVE
Climb That Mountain!

Eighth grade and early teens take their own peculiar toll in many families. A time of growth, physical and emotional, with the beginnings of cutting the apron strings from parents, youngsters in this age group frequently spend most days in some sort of turmoil. They are neither mature nor experienced enough to handle many of the problems facing them.

Peer pressure from every direction to buy drugs, buy cigarettes, experiment with sex and alcohol, skip school, bring knives, guns and other weapons to school, join gangs, be accepted, fight students and teachers, lie, cheat, steal…the list is endless and getting longer.

The difficulties that David encountered with other students continued. However, occasionally he was able to build some self-confidence that made his days a bit easier.

He developed an interest in science, not surprising since he'd been around veterinary medicine all of his life. Anna Southard appreciated both the person and the potential of David. Somehow, almost miraculously, she shared our hopes for David's future. In fact, her insight, coupled with her great love of children, led her to invite David into her "regular" eighth grade English and science classes at Texico.

What a gigantic step, because David was now competing in the classroom with "normal" children and doing it successfully!

During the spring semester, he entered a project..."How Rockets are Formed"...in the science fair, carefully constructing two model rockets and writing up the information on his project.

One of the rockets was detonated, for a photo op, and to get the statistics on how far and how high it traveled. What a momentous afternoon, as the onlookers included one of our ministers who was an enthusiast of rocket science, plus a junior high math teacher and his wife, plus an engineer, George and myself.

George and the math teacher handled the more sophisticated equipment so that we could accurately detail the height and width of travel, while David and the pastor did the actual preparations. David launched his rocket and all of the information and pictures became part of the project.

When we went to school to place David's entry with the hundred others, I couldn't help wondering, "What will he think if he doesn't do as well as he expects?"

He'd been saying for two months that his project would win! He simply knew it.

And, furthermore, he believed it!

I felt that he had done exceptionally well, diligently working on it, but I didn't want him to become overconfident and perhaps very disappointed. "Parent" and "protective" are often synonymous, and they described me—perfectly!

Anyhow, George and I cautioned him, "Son, you've done great work, but so have a lot of other students. Don't be too disappointed if you don't win. After all, everyone has worked hard."

So much for our faith, which was—to put it charitably—somewhat less than his!

The judging was done after school with entries identified only by number, not by name. The results were finally revealed the following day. I walked into the gym in mid-afternoon, saw David with a huge grin, standing near his project, and I could see from across the floor that there was a blue ribbon hanging on his entry!

I ran up to him and hugged him. "David, I know you're so happy about this...and so am I! and isn't Mrs. Southard proud of you, too?"

I looked around as Bill Southard, Anna's husband and editor of the *Clovis News Journal*, reached out to shake hands with David and congratulate him.

"Thanks, Mr. Southard. I'm sure pleased."

"By the way, Mom, what about this?" he asked, as he handed me a plaque that noted:

Texico High School
Junior Division
Science Fair 1983
RESERVE CHAMPION

I couldn't believe my eyes! Not only did he have a first-place blue ribbon, but also he'd won reserve champion, which meant he could take his entry to the district science fair in a few weeks!

"George, you're not gonna believe this," I called out excitedly, as we returned to the clinic, "but David has some wonderful news for you!"

"Hey, Dad, look at these," he simply glowed as he produced the ribbon and plaque. "What do you think now?"

"Son, I think you were right, all along. You did have a winning project...and I'm so proud of you!"

No, he didn't win the district competition, but the experience was memorable and marked another positive milestone for him.

He'd just recently completed several other milestones, being named in fifth place out of forty students in one of his combined seventh and eighth grade classes. For a U.S. history test, he'd correctly named all forty presidents, their parties, home states and years of service, after days and nights of dogged training and memorization. I showed him how to do the work in a pattern so that he could remember it...it worked and so did he!

On the heels of that accomplishment, he memorized Lincoln's Gettysburg address after at first trying to convince himself that it would be impossible...and he did superbly on the oral exam.

After the science project, his teacher Mrs. Southard called us one evening to share the news that David had been given the only "A+" in her class for the past two days, for continually correctly answering her science questions.

She commented that David's grades chagrined the "normal" students and she laughingly commented that his classmates were openly envious of his efforts. Our smiles seemed to expand with each remark she made.

The end of the school year brought another awards assembly highlight for David. He received certificates for being the "Most Improved 8th Grade U.S. History Student" and for a "Special Science Award" complete with a medal.

The evening of junior high graduation, he proudly took his place with the other students, decked out in his new slacks and jacket, looking so grown up and accepting the congratulations of peers, teachers and parents.

Another mountain had just been climbed with more peaks daring us on the horizon.

May 1983 was full of busy projects for all of us.

Remodeling part of the clinic into an apartment, we welcomed the first tenant, nineteen-year-old Cindy Tallman, daughter of George's cousins Richard and Beverly Tallman of Tulsa. Cindy was to live there while she worked in the clinic for two months as she considered a career in veterinary medicine. Having completed her first year at OSU, she was still looking for a major.

Cindy's arrival coincided with an end-of-school gathering John had for a few of the NMMI cadets. He'd called a couple of weeks earlier, asking about bringing some friends home for a weekend. "Certainly," I said, "just let me know how many and when."

"Some" turned out to be more than twenty!

It was a wonderful weekend and fun for all of us as well as quite a start to the summer!

In June, George and I spent eighteen days on a long-anticipated trip to Egypt, Greece and the Holy Land.

The three teenagers were left to fare for themselves, which they managed to do. John, newly turned seventeen and David, approaching fifteen, followed their dad's suggestion and bought paint (of their color choice and matching nothing else on the premises!) and proceeded to do an almost perfect job of painting the 1,780-square-foot detached garage.

George had spent two years in his very limited spare time building the three-car garage/shop and, finally, it looked finished. We were greatly impressed when we returned, both by the quality of their work and to see that both boys were maturing. They could be trusted to carry out the promise to behave (most of the time), take care of the house and stay gainfully busy in our absence.

John's return to New Mexico Military Institute in August, as a (high school senior) fourth-year cadet, was followed a week later by David's entry into Texico High School as a freshman. The annual trauma soon followed.

At John's insistence, and against what George and I felt was our better judgment, David joined workouts for the football team. He'd never participated in organized sports except from the sidelines, and we now wondered about the advisability of it.

David's gross motor skills were still far behind those of his peers…running was a chore, to say nothing of catching or throwing a ball…plus learning the plays. However, we gave in…and away he went!

"Mom, I'm too sore and tired to eat."

What a shock!

David had never been *too anything* to eat!

Practice had started three days earlier, and, manfully, David was doing the best he could to cooperate with the coaches. Ninth graders still played on the junior high team…and at five feet nine inches and 165 pounds, David towered over—and around—most of the players for Texico, as well as their opponents!

If sheer player-volume could win games, David was headed for a good season. In a small school such as Texico, there was virtually no competition for being selected as a team member…all warm bodies with a heart rate and functioning lungs were needed and suited up…which added to our son's soaring confidence in himself.

He was on the team and suiting up for games…even if he didn't play a whole lot.

And, in Texico's emerald and white uniform, he resembled a close copy of the Jolly Green Giant!

Mom learned, to her extreme dismay, that the school did not launder either practice or game uniforms. From August until November when the final game whistle was blown, our washing machine obligingly turned his stained, sweaty gear into nearly acceptable garb five nights a week, while his shoulder and leg pads and shoes dried in front of the floor fan.

After years of rejection, David was starting to feel more a part of the group at school, and, for a few weeks both his outlook and his disposition zoomed upward.

We received no complaints from the teachers or administrators. Even at Parents' Night in October, assurances were given that all was well.

By December, though, David began to be more easily distracted and much less cooperative at home, eventually returning to his hyperactive behavior and emotional outbursts.

When we questioned him, he'd reply, "The kids hate me," or "I hate myself," or "I can't stand going to school anymore!" Mystified by his actions, we tried to find out what was happening and we were told that he was being disruptive in class, argumentative, not paying attention and discussing topics of unacceptable social situations when teachers would leave the room.

Looking to David for answers was the equivalent of talking to the wall. He had never been a person who would easily share his deepest hurts. The more we asked, the less we heard.

The semester finally ended and all we were told by our son was that "the kids keep teasing me, calling me all kinds of terrible names and trying to get me to talk about things that I know I shouldn't talk about."

The worst was yet to come: Semester grades arrived after several weeks of David's dallying about bringing home his report cards...and George and I paled at the revelation: He was either failing, or near-failing, in almost every subject!

All semester I'd asked him every day about his homework, and he always assured both his dad and me that he'd "completed it at school because the teacher doesn't want me to bring it home."

?

And, he was telling the truth.

His most difficult subjects, math and English, were done in the "special education resource room" with a special education instructor. He was failing those! How does a person fail special education?

We wondered, more than once, how could this happen...when the class was specially structured (or supposed to be) to meet the needs of the students...and was taught, we were told, by master's-degree-level instructors who could recognize the deficiencies and help the students meet those needs.

Something dreadful had gone awry during the semester while we innocently stood by, uninformed about it. The teacher actually did not want David to take homework out of the school building, because she had discovered that I would help him with it.

Not do it for him, but help him.

I helped him to the point of making him re-do entire pages of math so that they looked neat and ready to hand in.

The same thing occurred in English.

His verbal skills still far outweighed his written abilities, and we had spent hours working on his papers...David telling me what he was trying to express...and I helping him spell words correctly, use the proper grammar and punctuation.

I helped and encouraged, but did not do his work. The teacher, early in the semester, saw that when he took work home he made good grades on it...not because someone was doing it for him, but because he was receiving the one-on-one assistance that he needed.

It followed, that if he had good grades on his homework then his over-all average would be increased and that would show up on his report card.

To our disgust, we found that the Texico superintendent did not want that to happen!

It appeared that this man, with whom we had experienced a royal encounter at the beginning of David's first semester in eighth grade, had somehow communicated, either by hints or outright directives, that "David Kendall is to make low grades…in order that his parents will hopefully remove him from our school!"

We talked to numerous people, including Texico teachers and aides, as well as administrative people in the Clovis system, who informed us that they had known all along of this problem!

The Texico superintendent had become incensed that we had caught him in lies about his school board not wanting Clovis students to ride the Texico buses. We had discussed the problem with the State of New Mexico school officials, who called the superintendent's hand on it. His furious reaction resulted in the dramatic drop in David's grades.

"Why didn't you tell us…say something sooner?" we asked those who knew of the situation.

"I didn't want to upset you."

"I couldn't…I didn't want to cause problems for you or for myself. After all, I have to work in the Texico system."

"I'm so sorry for all of you, Carolyn…you and George and David. I knew what was happening…we all did…"

And on and on. Expressions of regret coming much too little and far too late.

There were, also, expressions of regret for a kicking incident involving several students, both girls and boys, at school. David told us that several kids were attempting to stuff him into a dumpster and during the struggle one of the girls had kicked him—hard—in the groin. He experienced a great deal of pain and nothing was done to punish the other students, although the principal had the audacity to call and tell us we needed to pay (?) for the bloody nose David gave the girl who kicked him. She came into the line of fire with his fist when she was pushing on him, trying to get him inside the dumpster, and he was thrashing around.

We thought that the pain had subsided when he no longer mentioned it and the subject didn't come up again until three years later, the spring of 1987 when David finally showed his dad why he was always in terrible pain, although he never mentioned it. To put on underwear and jeans was so painful that it was almost more than he could tolerate.

The problem was due to a hydrocele, an inflamed testicle, the result of the kicking incident. It was necessary for David to have surgery at Lubbock Methodist Hospital to repair the problem and ease the pain (and embarrassment) he'd suffered for three years.

Once our eyes were opened about the Texico superintendent, and when I had finished crying and George had finished hollering, we approached the Clovis system to see if there would be a place for David. The Texico superintendent wanted him out...and out we would take him!

Once again, Carolyn Luck shared her friendship, her expertise and her authority as head of Clovis Special Education. In spite of a demanding professional schedule that normally prevented her being able to personally test students, she took the time and did the evaluation work on David.

As it happened, this was the year for his tri-annual, in-depth work up by the school system, and her excitement was contagious when Carolyn called after grading the tests: "I can't believe it," she bubbled, "David has come such a long way and I'm so thrilled for him!"

"What do you mean?" I asked, although I felt sure that I already knew what her reply would be.

"He shows such improvement in most areas that it's hard to believe this is the same student we tested three years ago!

"We went through all of the work for his grade level, then just kept right on going. Did you know that in some areas he's testing several years ahead?"

"No, but I'm not surprised," I managed to insert between her replays of the morning's events.

"He was answering all sorts of questions that *I* didn't know the answers to, such as what is DNA and how is it important to the body. I'm so proud of him and I know that things will go well for him, back here in Clovis. I believe that he's matured a great deal socially and emotionally, and should not have problems adapting to a larger school system. I'm making an appointment for you, George, David and me to talk to the Yucca Junior High principal and the counselor, so that we can get him enrolled and into the Clovis system right away."

Less than a week later, David was withdrawn (much to the pleasure of the Texico principal and the superintendent) and started classes at Yucca. What had unnerved us two weeks earlier was ending on a happier, hopeful note.

We asked for and received from the Yucca staff a sharing of viewpoints on his academic progress and problems.

Grades began to show improvement in spite of the fact that Dave was getting a several-weeks-late start on class work. Things did go well enough that by the end of the semester he was enrolled in high school classes and looking forward to the fall term.

The only serious problem during the semester wasn't with David, but with a young teacher, who was arrested at school for selling drugs to students while they were at school. He was David's English instructor and when I first heard his name, I thought David would be better off with someone else, as he was the son of the former Clovis superintendent and his nurse-wife who had caused so much misery for us! However, David was only in his class for three days before the man was arrested and Dave had a new teacher.

Clovis High, home of the Wildcats ("The Beast from the East") would be the largest school David had attended with a student body of approximately 1,600. As the fall semester approached, we began to get uneasy feelings that perhaps it would be too large for him to attend. We decided, with the assistance once again of Carolyn Luck plus the staff of Westbrook Christian School, that perhaps he should attend there, at least for one semester.

As it turned out, he made straight A's and the honor roll!

Second semester he enrolled as a sophomore at Clovis High.

CHAPTER TWENTY-SIX
In the Beginning…

Westbrook, very small classes with individualized instruction, was a good, although brief, experience for him.

Moving up to CHS gave both George and me butterflies, while David simply anticipated bigger and better opportunities! It's all in the attitude!

He would require very little of the special education classes and have an opportunity to be in "normal" classrooms with youngsters who probably had never faced problems anywhere as serious as his.

Of course, every day didn't go smoothly, and there remained much of the expected reaction to his being different. Some kids liked him…some didn't…some tolerated him, others openly and vocally showed their hate for him. Not much different that the reactions "normal" children had to each other.

However, good things began to happen immediately. When he'd been at CHS about a week, the counselor called me. She could, no doubt, tell from my response when I heard who was calling, that I must have been thinking, "Lord, what's happened this time?"

"Did David tell you that he was trying out for vocal music?"

"No."

He had acted rather strangely over the weekend, but had not mentioned a word about trying out for anything.

"Well," the counselor began, "he tried out today and Mr. Anderson was so pleased about him that he wants him in choir! We're really proud of him and wanted you to know it!"

You're proud of him? Us, too! Excited? Of course!

So many students tried out for choral groups and were unable to be accepted. The fact that David had done it, and had done it all by himself, pleased us to the point where we wanted to shout it from the roof tops! The first time that we saw him on stage in his tuxedo, singing his heart out and carefully watching ever move the director made, thrilled us. In fact, we videotaped nearly every performance!

The autumn of his senior year, he tried out for all-state choir...didn't make it, but at least he tried, and we felt that was the important part of the matter. He had the opportunity to go to Arizona and to Six Flags Over Texas for choral competition, making trips just like any other teenager.

During the spring, the II (excellent) that he earned on his first vocal solo competition immensely pleased all of us.

In December 1986, he was one of eight CHS students who attended "Close Up" in Washington D.C., for a week's look at Congress and how it operated. He had the chance to attend a session of the Supreme Court while they were hearing a case and he saw many of the tourist attractions, being especially impressed with the somber rites at Arlington Cemetery.

What an experience...and all of this from our young man who was never supposed to be able to go to school!

He had other opportunities to make trips with teens from church and school, sometimes being treated with less than respect by peers, but at six feet, 200 pounds, his size commanded some amount of respect! He appeared large enough to whip a bear with a stick, but that belied his gentle character.

David amazed us with the outcome of some of his more harrowing experiences. Back in October 1985, he was struck by a hit-and-run driver while he was on his bicycle, crossing the intersection, at our home. At the time he was probably 165 pounds and that weight and muscle might have been in his favor.

Two drivers, who saw the accident and told us about it, said that the vehicle that hit David knocked our son and his bike higher than the top of the automobile that struck him...then David hit the hood of the car, slid toward the windshield, fell off the car and onto the pavement!

He wasn't killed because God had other things for David to do!

The accident occurred on a five-lane highway, with lots of traffic including eighteen-wheelers. Thank God, none of them ran over him!

He landed on the side of his head, suffering a concussion and severe headache. However, rather than tell us what had happened, he pushed his smashed bike the short distance home, laid it against the side of the house, went inside and laid down in his room.

A few minutes after he walked inside, I happened to walk out and was met by the sickening sight of the mutilated bicycle. Quizzed about what happened to it, he told us about the car hitting him, assuring us that he was "feeling O.K." He had a few scrapes and bruises, but kept saying that he didn't want to go to the hospital, didn't want x-rays, and he would "be alright…don't worry about me."

After weeks of supposedly searching for the car and driver, the police told us they had nothing to report. We had driven around the area and found a car that David said was the one that hit him, but nothing was done about it.

After a few weeks, he began to complain that he was not seeing well. As he already wore glasses, we thought that might be part of the problem. I took him to the Texas Tech University Teaching Hospital at Lubbock, ophthalmology department.

After four hours of a thorough exam, it was agreed among the doctors that David had a tear in the retina on the side of his head that had hit the pavement.

Following five minutes and $900 in front of the laser, the repair was complete and he was not expected to have any further problems with the injury. Thankfully, he was no longer playing contact sports or he might have had very serious problems with another hard blow to his head. In fact, the doctors said that another hard knock could have completed the tear, allowing the fluid from the back of his eye to flow forward, blinding him permanently in that eye!

At the age of sixteen, David discovered the sometimes-dubious joy of vehicle ownership. He'd worked in our veterinary hospitals since he was quite young. We had forced him to save part of his earnings and put them into something that would accumulate interest.

After he passed driver's ed, he found to his delight that he had enough money saved to purchase a good, used pickup, as well as pay for his own gas and insurance. Earlier, he'd purchased a $99-car that he used to do his practice driving on the empty seven acres next door to us.

Round and round, up, back, into ditches, into mud, getting a bit of experience before he took off on the real roads, which he soon tackled like a pro. No accidents, no tickets. A better car-driving history than his older brother...

Following a fund-raising event for the CHS choral groups, an award was named for David, as he set a record for the most money ever raised during their candy sale. To our knowledge, the award is still given each spring to the top salesperson.

At the beginning of his senior year, he brought home information concerning the ACT tests for college. After he looked it over, he said, "Mom, do you suppose that I should just forget about it?"

"No, I don't think you should forget about it. I think that if you want to take it, then take it as many times as you care to. You'll never know what you can do, until you try!" That opinion, seconded by George, was all the encouragement he needed.

Certainly, there were many things on the test that he had not the smallest exposure to, including any sort of higher mathematics. However, George and I told him that it would be pretty unusual if a student knew all of the answers to all of the questions...and he should just do the best that he could.

He took it...he passed...not with a tremendously high score...but he passed on the first try!

Dave graduated with a GPA over 3.0 and without being in any Special Ed class his senior year. He managed to astound his dad and me—and others— by making A's and B's in biology with one of the most difficult science teachers at CHS and after memorizing complicated genetic charts.

Our precious other son, John, sometimes was very gruff with David as they matured, to the point of using Dave's head as a battering ram on his bedroom wall, leaving a hole that was covered for years with only a picture, as we awaited the next brotherly confrontation. However, John also showed an understanding and tenderness that was heartwarming.

Two of the very special moments that I remember were when John took David to see the movie, *Rainman*, then couldn't sit all the way through it, identifying so closely with the characters. David, on the other hand, didn't have many of the problems of the leading character, Raymond, but there was a heart-tugging similarity between John and the older brother played by Tom Cruise, whom John also physically resembled.

The other memorable event was David's twenty-seventh birthday which was hosted in Dallas by John. David was treated to a special time of shopping for new clothes, a trip to the stylist (a first for Dave) for a new haircut with beard/moustache trim...plus dining out, of course!

David, beaming, wearing his new suit and seated beside John at the restaurant, bears witness to the grand weekend in Big D...and it probably was a lot more fun than another birthday weekend for him in Dallas when he, George and I flew there for his fifteenth.

In 1990, The Foundation for Exceptional Children presented David the "Yes! I Can" award for "Independent Living Skills" at an impressive meeting in Toronto, Canada, before an audience of more than 500 parents and friends. The thirty-five other young recipients of a variety of awards were selected from more than 1,400 entrants. The winners ranged from five to twenty-one years of age with disabilities covering the spectrum of birth defects/brain damage.

David's award acknowledged his ability to live alone, care for himself and attend college...more than 100 miles from his parents...overturning the bad predictions, forecasts and diagnoses made during his earlier life.

Following a welcome party the night before the awards, we went to dinner. David was literally beside himself with a surprise for us that he alternately wanted to share, then wanted to keep to himself for a few more minutes. We wondered what he was thinking!

Finally, he said, "Mom and Dad, I have something to tell you. The other kids want me to be their spokesperson tomorrow, to thank everyone for the awards!"

WOW!

Luckily, David had taken a public speaking course the previous semester at Eastern New Mexico University and he was awake nearly all night, collecting his thoughts and putting them on paper...without letting us know what he was going to say. He silently practiced, over and over, en route to the awards presentation, still without giving us a clue about his speech.

During the presentation of awards, children walked, cautiously stumbled on crutches, rode in wheelchairs across the stage, or were led by a parent if the child happened to be blind, while the moderator announced that particular child's achievement. Each youngster was given a wonderful bronze sculpture made by a New Mexico artist, himself blinded on the Viet Nam battlefield. The artist shook hands and smiled warmly as he congratulated each winner, even though he could not see who was receiving one of his statues.

When it was time, after children of all ages and disabilities had been honored for their marvelous accomplishments, David stood before the expectant auditorium, all eyes and TV cameras on him, and said, "I want to thank all of you for coming today to our awards. I want to thank parents and families, especially my parents and family, for their love, their patience and care, for helping me to learn and grow and be able to get this award. Most of all, I want to thank God for His help!"

The auditorium burst in applause and cheers; people were on their feet, clapping, whistling and shouting!

David was so startled that he took a step backward, then, slowly smiled and accepted the outburst of praise from parents, friends, relatives and well-wishers, waving to the audience like a seasoned politician; shaking hands with the moderators and other recipients on stage.

Our hearts nearly burst!

Thinking back over the years since this story began, there are many memories that come to mind, recalling David's journey and I'm grateful for them.

He still lives and works in Roswell, New Mexico, where he accumulated approximately 110 hours of college credit with a GPA of 2.6. He did this taking classes mostly concerning the art that he loves. With his artistic gift, he has found a great deal of pleasure in drawing, painting and sculpting.

One of our treasures is a picture of a lovely lady, drawn by David, framed and hanging above my desk, adding beauty to our office…reminding me every time I look up at it, how grateful I am for David and for John. What a blessing to be their mother, "Abuela" to our grandsons and wife to George.

There are, of course, many things that may never be David's, nor mine, nor George's, nor John's, nor our two young grandsons, Will and Max Kendall.

What is David's is our deep and abiding love and our respect for his spirit of never giving up!

What is David's is the knowledge that this manuscript is only the beginning of his story!

"**Nevertheless**, not my will, but Thine be done."

Printed in the United States
83815LV00002B/706-795/A